Why This Book Was Written

This is a book for everyone - from an individual who needs to effectively manage their own stress, to a manager, supervisor or team leader who has to deal quickly with any stress-related problems in the workplace.

The format of the book is one that delivers practical answers to the many questions we all have about how to manage stress to achieve a healthy work-life balance.

Full of proven tips and strategies, this book will leave the reader feeling confident that they can handle stress in a way that will deal not only with the effects of excessive pressure on personal performance and relationships, but also with the root of the problem.

The tools, skills and techniques presented, are based on Carole's experience over twenty five years in managing workplace stress as she shares with you the secrets of how to overcome its damaging effects, whether at home or at work.

Read the book from cover to cover, or dip into it when you have a stress-related problem that needs solving quickly! Its aim is to deliver instant answers to your questions.

Either way, keep it close to hand so that you can **Show Stress Who's Boss!**

*In memory of my darling Mother, Peggy,
who overcame her life's challenges and
passed on her courage and determination
to her three children*

What Fellow Authors Say

"You have to look a long way to find a book of practical anti-stress measures that are immediately usable by HR specialists and general management alike. This book exactly fulfils its claims - a toolbox of skills and techniques for managing those familiar workplace pressures that too easily harden into stress. It is written with the easy confidence of an experienced counsellor who is also a successful businesswoman, presented in a less-usual format, and spiced with humour. You can tell you are in the hands of someone who cares deeply about healthy workplace culture." *Hani Soubra, Regional Director, BBC World, MENA, Dubai. Author of 'Letters to Dahlia.'*

"As a writer and presenter on networking, I know as well as anyone the importance of being in a totally de-stressed state in order to exploit a networking opportunity to the full. 'Show Stress Who's Boss' manages to simplify the subject of stress management without any loss of essential content. In particular, the book includes a most useful 'manager's toolbox' that takes the newcomer straight to an authoritative position from which to manage the workplace pressures that can turn to stress." *Jan Vermeiren, Author of 'How to REALLY Use LinkedIn'.*

"Carole's comprehensive guide to managing stress is brimming with anecdotes, stories and practical solutions which make it easily accessible, effortlessly readable and eminently enjoyable to anyone interested in this fascinating topic. I cannot suggest a better guide than Carole Spiers to help you navigate your way through stress." *Damian Hughes, founder of Change Management consultancy LiquidThinker, and author of 'Liquid Thinking', 'Liquid Leadership' and 'The Survival Guide to Change'.*

"In her new book 'Show Stress Who's Boss', Carole Spiers clearly ticks all the boxes of the optimistic iCan philosophy which is my own speciality as a motivational speaker. So let Carole show you that 'You Can', by reading this book, which is the product of twenty years' notable success in the stress counselling and consultancy business. That's a mass of professional wisdom condensed into one highly readable and usable work. It'll probably turn out a best-seller in its class. Or is it in a class of its own?" *Richard McCann, No 1 Bestselling Author of 'Just a Boy'.*

"'Show Stress Who's Boss' makes the perfect companion volume to my own life-balance book 'Slow Down to Speed Up', and I wish I'd written it myself. The different ways that pressure can build up are charted and illustrated with wonderful clarity. And the stress management skills are presented like a high-class tutorial that will equip you to start combating stress the moment you've finished reading." *Lothar Seiwert, Keynote Speaker and Author of 'Slow Down to Speed Up', www.seiwert.de.*

"I always knew that Stress Management had a lot to do with my own speciality of Time Management. But I never saw the issue so well-explained and clearly set out. This book has not only re-affirmed much of the professional wisdom of the HR

department, but taught me new lessons too. Yet it's presented in a style that's accessible to the general reader, and I've already recommended it to a number of my coaching clients." *Robyn Pearce, author of 'Getting a Grip on Time' and four other time-related titles.*

Comments from Fellow Professionals

"It's rare and very refreshing to read a book that is so direct, clear and so evidently useful. In 'Show Stress Who's Boss' Carole takes the reader through practical case studies and examples to illustrate her down-to-earth advice and her 'toolbox' of methods and tips for improvement. Carole inspired our senior board with her stress management training course and her advice to us has been invaluable through the challenging times of the financial crisis. This book will certainly be required reading for our senior team as the tools and strategies she describes are vital for effective team management and the building of a sustainable business." *Andrew Shaw, CEO, Dubai Cables.*

"This book is like an extension of Carole's popular weekly stress column in Gulf News. It represents the fruit of 20 years at the top of the stress management business, and these valuable tools and strategies can be used anywhere on earth. Stylistically, the book is a good blend of formal tuition and informal tips, and I have recommended it to my executives at all levels. For me personally, it is one of the few manuals I keep permanently out on the desk for daily consultation." *Mohamed Ahmed Al-Muflehi HSM (ADMA HSEQAD).*

"This excellent book is full of useful stress busting strategies and techniques. They are simple to apply in many situations including the workplace." *Prof Stephen Palmer PhD. Director: Centre for Stress Management, London*

"Everyone who endures the cruel effects of stress at work or at home has been crying out for an inspirational book that sets out clearly how to banish the curse of modern living. Thank

Thank You to...

My valued team at the Carole Spiers Group who always give 100%.

Michael who corrects my copy, and me.

Andrea for her professional input and guidance.

Dennis who brought my cartoons to life.

Chris and his team at Filament Publishing.

All the people who have sent me stories and quotations over many years.

" *When we dream, it's only a dream. When we dream together, it is the beginning of reality. I would like to thank those of you who share my dream.* **"**

Carole Spiers

Preface by

Cary L. Cooper, CBE, Professor of Organizational Psychology and Health at Lancaster University Management School, President of the British Association of Counselling and Psychotherapy and co-author of 'How to Deal with Stress' (Kogan Page, London).

Nelson Mandela once said 'the greatest glory in living lies not in never failing, but in rising every time we fail'.

With the increasing pressures on people at work in a global, competitive, ever changing and less secure world of today, managing the stress of work and life are fundamental to people's wellbeing and to the performance of our businesses.

There are many aspects of work in the 21st Century which are profoundly different from decades past; intrinsic job insecurity, heavier workloads contributed to by new technology (e.g. emails, laptops, mobile technology), the increased global mobility away from protective communities and the extended family, longer working hours, the spilling over of work into family and one's personal life, and the ever faster pace of decision making and business life generally.

This book will help you focus in on the main aspects of workplace stress, providing you with a useful profile to help you identify and deal with these 'stressors', both as an individual and as a manager.

It is important for organisations to understand that stress at work can damage their bottom line, as well as the health and wellbeing of their employees.

People are motivated by other things than just money. They also crave a good quality of working life, or as Studs Terkel commented in his book **Working** *'work is about a search for daily meaning as well as daily bread, for recognition as well as cash, for astonishment rather than torpor, in short, for a sort of life rather than a Monday through Friday sort of dying'.*

Foreword by

Dr. Saeed M. Al Barwani
Dubai, UAE

The Middle East and especially the UAE is at the forefront of ever growing change and adaptation, in a rich cauldron full of multinationals - all working in a seamless yet different business environment with a variety of business ethics, standards and cultures.

We live in a culture where tomorrow's achievements are wanted yesterday, with double or treble growth, and where 'impossible' does not exist and where change is the only visible constant. This change in its visible sense is an assurance of normal UAE life. I cannot imagine the UAE without growth or change. Its evolving landscape and values never cease to amaze many people and yet attract more people into this exciting environment. This makes me feel humble and proud to be an Emirati in these times.

Not so many years ago, we used to enjoy a working day that stretched from 7 am to 2 pm, where siesta was a norm and time with family and friends was taken for granted. Little did we know that the new norm would be a never ending day that is interspersed by sleep in the late hours of the night, and preoccupied by business and networking circles. Faces and new faces from all over the world are the order and theme of our lives.

Organisations new and old are faced with the challenges of growth in the region, organisations that have to adopt industrialised ways to survive and compete, and as a result this takes a toll on the people.

With this diversity and culture, working people and their families live through challenging times where management of people of different backgrounds and standards are also a norm in start-up and new organisations. Families are transplanted from a secure extended network of family support into insular living conditions where the working person is faced with new challenges at work and even newer challenges at home in this new land and environment.

Stresses, tensions and new working environment are a theme for the new people in the UAE, as well as for those who have been in the region for many years, since they also experience these challenges as the old comfortable world is constantly getting shaken to its core.

There is no better time to introduce Carole's book into the region, as a practical and useful tool for Managers, Supervisors, Welfare staff and HR/HC communities to help them identify, deal with and resolve stress via examples, checklists and templates.

The book makes light reading, with its many relevant quotes from famous people and a rich list of other related reference material.

Contents

Step 3: Getting to Grips 73

How To:

Step 4: Regaining Control   133

Changing Behaviour   136

How to:

Changing Your Mindset 209

How to:

Additional Stress-Busting Resources 217

Introduction

I am writing this book with employers under more financial pressure than ever, and managers having to manage greater problems with fewer resources. But you don't have to wait for a bad year to make good use of proven stress management techniques.

Over the last 20 years, businesses both large and small, have retained me to deliver stress management training to their senior executives and management teams. This book summarises my experiences and conclusions about the management of everyday workplace pressures, in order to successfully prevent them hardening into stress.

Stress management is mostly to do with being able to recognise signs of stress in oneself and others, and developing effective anti-stress techniques to deal promptly with it. Whilst stress is often perceived as being workplace or financially-oriented, you will see that it can dramatically affect home and family life.

With the aid of this book, you will learn the basic tools and techniques of managing stress and hopefully become a better manager, colleague and family member.

Here's to your stress-free living!

Carole Spiers

How to Get the Most Out of This Book

Stress Management:
An Intelligent Personal and Professional Investment

This book will give you instant access to strategies and tools for you to include within your portfolio of management skills. The **"HOW TO"** tools in this book provide solution based skills to help you deal with specific problems and challenges that you may encounter on a day to day basis.

The aim of this book is to:

1. Help you to identify your personal stress levels and give you the necessary tools to manage them more effectively.
2. Learn how to recognise stress in others and how to offer help to reduce it.
3. Discover the causes and effects of stress.
4. Develop personal management skills which, if used regularly, will help reduce your stress and the stress within your teams.

" *A journey of a thousand miles must begin with a single step!* **"**

Lao-Tzu

Some of the techniques described may be familiar whilst for others, they may be new. What is obvious to one person is not necessarily obvious to another. Additionally, just because we are aware of a skill or technique does not automatically mean that we utilise it, successfully or at all, in our lives at home and at work.

Most workplace pressure is a usual and often positive part of working life, motivating you to achieve a better and more effective performance. However, when pressure becomes excessive and prolonged, it can turn into stress and become destructive, resulting in a spiral of unpleasant feelings and behaviour.

Over time stress can affect your mental and physical wellbeing leading to your work performance falling well below your natural ability and leaving you feeling unable to cope with normal activity.

Relationships at home and at work can also be seriously affected by stress. Your own stresses can reduce your ability to manage your team effectively, and your personal relationships may become strained.

" *Begin at the beginning,' the King said very gravely, 'and go on till you come to the end: then stop.* "

Lewis Carroll

STEP 1
Spotting the Symptoms

" Sometimes when people are under stress, they hate to think, and it's the time when they most need to think. "

Bill Clinton

True or False – the Facts About Stress

There are many myths and misconceptions about stress that could cause you significant damage if you base your life on such inaccuracies.

Three of the most commonly quoted include the following.

1. 'Stress is Good for You'

It is often mistakenly thought that stress is good for people, when in fact long-term stress is invariably harmful. A certain amount of pressure can indeed motivate and can therefore be useful, but stress is never so.

A probable explanation of the myth that people perform well under stress is that they perform well under controlled pressure, i.e. when that pressure is effectively managed.

Pressure is useful when the body and mind are finely tuned in a way that enables them to achieve optimum results and performance. A feeling of nervousness before giving a presentation will often result in increased mental acuity and responsiveness, which will also stimulate the audience. The relevant factor in this context is 'pressure' that is within your control.

However, if you arrived late, inadequately prepared, and the laptop or projector failed to operate properly, then the presentation would inevitably be stressful.

> The word 'stress' itself is often applied incorrectly. Many people will use it when they have a temporary work overload, whereas in fact, stress only occurs when a person perceives (over a prolonged period) that he or she has insufficient personal resources to cope with a given situation.

We can think of stress as a light switch that our body turns on automatically under specific circumstances. The essence of effective stress management is the ability to know when (and how) to turn the switch off!

2. 'Suffering from Stress is a Sign of Weakness'

Individuals working in an organisation where, for example, there is the possibility of imminent redundancies, may seek to cover up any sign of stress in the belief that they may be regarded as unable to cope with their jobs and might therefore be regarded as expendable.

Employees may be wary of any mention of stress being attached to their work records in case it might prejudice their chances of promotion and so will not be inclined to discuss the problem with colleagues. This is why it is so important that workplace culture embraces the notion that to be stressed occasionally is a normal human condition and that to admit to it, initially to oneself, is the first step in modifying the situation or meeting the challenge.

> You may think that if you admit to being stressed, it is a sign of failure, weakness or ineptitude.

3. 'Stressors Affect Everybody Equally'

An employer or manager should appreciate that not all members of their team will react in the same way to any given problem. What one person perceives merely as pressure, another may perceive as stress.

Managers and supervisors need to be aware of the symptoms of stress and have the skills and expertise to defuse or mitigate such issues before they become potentially serious or disruptive.

The opportunity to talk through work-related problems and personal issues can help those employees who are under excessive pressure.

Whilst managers can often provide the first line of support in encouraging staff to take steps to combat the problem, it may be necessary to seek further support through an in-house referral, from either Human Resources, the line manager, Occupational Health Department or an external counselling service sponsored by the employer.

What Makes Events Stressful?

Negative events are more likely to be stressful than positive events -
although not exclusively so. Uncontrollable or unpredictable events are
more stressful than those that are not, and ambiguous situations are often
perceived as more stressful than those that are clear-cut.

Overworked people are invariably more stressed than those with fewer
tasks to perform and often have difficulty in balancing their home and work
lives. They frequently cannot set their priorities correctly and as a result may
only require something comparatively inconsequential to upset their
emotional balance.

> Your key aim should be to maintain an appropriate
> work-life balance, and that means (among other factors),
> making informed choices, setting priorities and
> employing effective time management techniques.

Exercise # 1

How Stressed Are You?

This simple questionnaire will give you an indication of your present stress level. Score each question with 3 for 'always', 2 for 'sometimes' or 1 for 'never'.

- [ ] I rarely allow enough time to complete tasks

- [ ] I seldom arrive for appointments on time

- [ ] I am impatient and interrupt when people talk slowly

- [ ] I get really cross and irritated when I have to queue

- [ ] I sometimes take on too many jobs at once

- [ ] I often miss meals and just eat snacks as I work

- [ ] My life is controlling me rather than me controlling my life

- [ ] I tend to always walk quickly

- [ ] I am inclined to drive faster than I should

- [ ] I am easily irritated by little things

- [ ] I criticise others rather than give positive feedback

- [ ] I do not seem to be able to relax and switch off, especially at night

- [ ] If I want a job done properly, I do it myself

- [ ] I am indecisive when it comes to making important decisions

- [ ] I tend to avoid parties and social events
- [ ] I will put off dealing with problems and hope they will go away
- [ ] I tend to internalise my anger when something or someone annoys me
- [ ] I am very competitive and try really hard to win when I play sport
- [ ] I want everything I do to be perfect
- [ ] I know I am in denial about my major problems

TOTAL:

See page 71 for your results.

Exercise # 2

Personal Stress Awareness

My definition of stress is…

_____

_____

_____

_____

_____

_____

_____

_____

Some of the stressors in my life, at home and work, are…

_____

_____

_____

_____

_____

_____

_____

_____

_____

Is Stress Good for You? No it's Not!

> **"** Stress is the adverse reaction people have to excess pressures or other types of demands placed on them. It arises when they perceive that they are unable to cope with those demands. **"**
>
> UK Health and Safety Executive (2001)

From the time of the hunter-gatherer, about two million years ago, stress has helped us to survive danger.

As soon as we perceive an impending threat to our safety, our possessions or our space, our brain sends messages to our nervous system to prepare to either stand and fight, or run to escape from the danger, i.e. 'fight or flight'.

Neolithic Man

When Neolithic Man went out to forage for food and came across a sabre-toothed tiger with the same intent, he had to make an instant decision to either fight with the beast (and possibly lose life or limb) or to make a quick escape.

In the split second that the body's fight/flight response was activated, the sympathetic nervous system would come into play and instantly kick-off the 'fight or flight' process.

These days, although we do not meet many tigers, we do meet a wide variety of threats in many other forms and when we are suddenly faced with a threat of danger, our innate survival reaction 'kicks-in' automatically as shown.

Repeated exposure to stress over a sustained period of time may mean that our body is less able to recover.
This may eventually lead to the development of a stress-related illness.

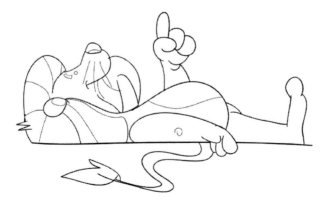

The challenges, threats and prolonged pressures we face today are often long-term rather than the instant ones that our forebears were likely to meet – and herein lies the difference.

We are probably more likely to be 'threatened' by late or delayed air travel, long hours, overwork, harassment, bullying or the thousand and one other causes of stress in our 21st Century workplace.

We currently live in a post-industrial period of transition, the so-called 'information age', which has introduced new technology systems and innovative management philosophies.

These have brought about very rapid changes in the workplace and increased expectations of those who work there.

Even the speed with which we are now expected to communicate via emails, mobile phones et al, leaves us little time for reflection before we are obliged to move swiftly on to the next task.

In addition to this, we are often required to work against a background of corporate mergers, short-term contracts, downsizing and possible redundancy which can pose very real threats to our day-to-day lives.

These developments clearly increase the incidence of stress, while on a personal level, should we be unable to cope with our work, any prolonged stress may influence the development of a wide range of medical complaints and diseases.

The Stress Process

" *It's not stress that kills us, it is our reaction to it.* "

Hans Selye

The word 'stress' itself possibly derives from the Latin 'strictus' meaning tight or narrow, or more likely from the Middle English 'stresse' meaning hardship or distress.

The originator of the biological concept of stress was the Nobel Prize winner Hans Selye, a Canadian physician and medical educator born in Austria – and a pioneer in the field of stress research.

Selye noted that a person who is subjected to prolonged stress goes through three phases: Alarm Reaction, Stage of Resistance and finally Exhaustion. He termed these responses the General Adaption Syndrome (GAS).

- **Alarm Reaction** is the 'fight or flight' response when the body's resources are mobilised and includes the various neurological and physiological responses that occur when confronted with a stressor – i.e. anything that causes excessive pressure to an individual, whether it be from external sources, interpersonal relationships or internal tensions.

- **Resistance:** If we continue to experience stress, the body enters the second stage, during which it is more able to cope with the original stress but its resistance to any other stress is lowered. If the threat is brief, there are usually sufficient reserves available to adapt.

- **Exhaustion:** After prolonged resistance, energy reserves are depleted and breakdown occurs. We do not have the energy to continue with the adaptation to the stress and the body fails to return to normal. Depending on the individual and the stressor, continued stress can lead to 'burnout' (breakdown), serious disease, organ failure or even death.

What Causes us to be Stressed?

- Fundamentally it is the way that we think about a situation rather than the situation itself that causes stress.

- Problems occur when the pressure we are under seems to be overwhelming or out of control. We may perceive ourselves as not possessing the necessary skills to combat the pressure, and so we feel unable to cope.

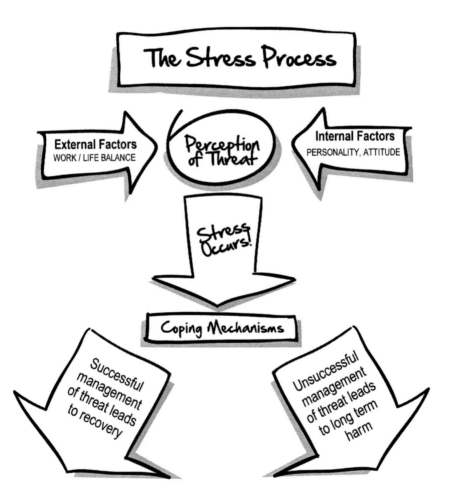

The Stress Process

External Factors
WORK / LIFE BALANCE

Perception of Threat

Internal Factors
PERSONALITY, ATTITUDE

Stress Occurs!

Coping Mechanisms

Successful management of threat leads to recovery

Unsuccessful management of threat leads to long term harm

Fig. 1

Case Study
Don't sweat the small stuff!

Craig and Molly are two Operations Managers who have each made appointments to meet their General Manager at one of their respective outlets.

Both encounter delays due to roadworks and an accident on the motorway. Both have mobile phones and they each let their boss know that they are going to be late. From there on, however, their reactions are totally different. Craig does all he can with the resources that are within his control. He listens to music on the radio and accepts that there is little he can do to get to his meeting any quicker.

Molly, on the other hand, grasps the steering wheel ever tighter, jumps from lane to lane in a desperate attempt to make up time and constantly looks at the clock, watching anxiously as the minutes tick by.

In the end, Molly arrives late and in a distressed and anxious state. Craig, on the other hand, arrives late but in a much more relaxed state of mind. Both were frustrated at being late but it is Molly who experiences high levels of stress.

As this example shows, innate resistance and reactions to stress vary from person to person.

> **"** Does anybody really think that they didn't get what they had because they didn't have the talent or the strength or the endurance or the commitment. **"**
>
> Nelson Mandela

Exercise # 3

How do You React when Experiencing Stress?

Think of a stressful situation that has taken place in the past. How did it affect you?

Psychologically, physically and emotionally.

For example, think back to the first time you had to give a presentation before an audience - how did you feel... how did your body react?

Situation

_____

_____

_____

How did it affect you?

_____

_____

_____

Think about how your reaction to this type of situation has changed over time, and what has influenced these changes?

_____

_____

_____

Personal Responses to Stress

A useful way of looking at stress is to examine it in terms of the three key types of responses through which it is expressed:

- Psychological – our mindset, how we think and feel.

- Physical – how our body reacts.

- Behavioural – how we perform and the signs we exhibit.

Psychological

The psychological symptoms associated with stress are relatively well known and most of us will have experienced them at one or more points in our lives. It is common, for example, to experience some anxiety before giving a major presentation or attending an important interview.

This is normal and soon passes once the event is over. What may be considered abnormal is a persistent feeling of anxiety that is experienced by many individuals who feel chronically stressed.

This anxiety may manifest itself in irritation, impatience or anger and in many cases leads to depression, a sense of hopelessness and other negative emotions.

Physical

In addition to its emotional impact, the adverse effects of stress on the physical health of an individual should not be underestimated. There is considerable research to suggest that there are links between stress and serious illness, some of which may influence life expectancy.

Stress can weaken the immune system, leading to an increased susceptibility to illnesses such as colds, flu and other infections, in addition to a raised blood pressure.

When stress is prolonged, there is a tendency for minor ailments to develop into more debilitating conditions – with migraine, irritable bowel syndrome and chest pains being amongst the most common.

Behavioural

It is not just the effects of physical illness that can impact on an individual's ability to perform their job. Stress invariably causes changes in individual behavioural patterns that may well prove to be disruptive in the workplace. Anger and frustration can also be triggered when individuals are unable to cope with pressure and these feelings can, in turn, impact on productivity and general morale.

A manager who is aggressive will fail to obtain the optimum output from his or her team members who are likely to become resentful and possibly stressed themselves. In this respect, stress is infectious and may be passed on from one person to another if appropriate action is not taken to identify and remedy the prime cause(s).

An intimidating management style or a culture of fear are just two of the factors contributing to the increased incidence of workplace bullying.

Individuals can become aggressive when they become frustrated or 'out of their depth' and this can often result in bullying behaviour being exhibited, from one level down to the next throughout a particular section of the organisation – or within the family unit.

For example, the normally calm manager may become frustrated and aggressive when put under pressure (supposedly to 'push' him or her to achieve the required results) and as a consequence, they may find it necessary to apply similar pressure to others at a subordinate level.

It is also important to appreciate that stress can, in some instances, turn the victims of bullying into bullies themselves both at work and at home.

Stress 'Carriers'

'Stress Carriers' are people, very often in a managerial or supervisory position, who have the ability to cause stress in others by intentionally raising the anxiety level of all those around them without suffering any adverse effect on themselves.

Their behaviour is often domineering and others are reluctant to confront them and invariably feel a sense of relief when not in their presence.

Case Study
Stress 'Carriers'

Helen, an office manager, is in charge of the dispatch section of an online retailing company. She manages her workload well but when Rema, her boss, comes into the office she finds that her schedule is completely thrown out by non-urgent tasks that Rema wants to be completed immediately. Rema's presence in the office creates an atmosphere of panic, and her unrealistic deadlines and lack of forward planning increase the working pressure throughout the department.

Rema herself, however, is confident of her method of management. If she can work under pressure then so can her team. 'People need extra challenges and it does them good to work under pressure. They need to be kept on their toes,' she says. She just cannot see that by upsetting work schedules with her often petty requests she is passing on her stress to the whole team.

Of course, anger and aggression are not the only behavioural symptoms of stress. Stress can also contribute towards an inability to concentrate, a weakening of essential focus and a difficulty in effectively managing time.

Whilst these effects may give some indication of the impact that stress can have on the individual, most people will only experience a limited number of these in response to any one particular stressor. Set out overleaf are some of the most commonly experienced warning signs of stress listed under either physical, emotional or behavioural (although this table itself is by no means exhaustive).

Physical, Emotional and Behavioural Effects of Stress

Depending on the individual, stress can manifest itself in different ways.

PHYSICAL	PSYCHOLOGICAL	BEHAVIOURAL
Palpitations, awareness of heart beating, chest pains	Mood swings	Susceptibility to accidents
Diarrhoea, constipation, flatulence	Panic attacks	Changes in eating habits
Indigestion	Morbid thoughts	Increased smoking
Loss of libido	Low self esteem	Restlessness, hyperactivity, foot tapping
Muscle tension	Irritability	Over-dependence on caffeine
Menstrual problems	Feeling of helplessness	Changes in sleep patterns
Tiredness	Impatience	Out of character behaviour
Breathlessness	Anxiety	Voluntary withdrawal from supportive relationships
Sweating	Crying	Disregard for personal appearance
Tightness in the chest	Cynicism	Loss of confidence

PHYSICAL	PSYCHOLOGICAL	BEHAVIOURAL
Skin and scalp irritation, eczema and psoriasis	Withdrawal into daydreams	Sullen attitude
Increased susceptibility to allergies	Intrusive thoughts or images	Clenched fists
Frequent colds, flu or other infections	Nightmares	Obsessive mannerisms
Rapid weight gain or loss	Suicidal feelings	Increased absence from work
Backache, neck pain	Paranoid thinking	Aggressiveness
Migraines and tension headaches	Guilt	Poor time management

Fig. 2   *Spiers C. Tolley's Managing Stress in the Workplace (2003)*

Case Study
Unhealthy Stress Response

Carrie is a 28 year old Sales Manager.

She has a young son and when she returns home it is important for her to spend time with him, in addition to having to manage the daily domestic chores.

Her store has recently been under scrutiny and several identifiable problems have emerged. It is Carrie's responsibility to resolve these difficulties, but she feels she is not getting the support from Head Office that she needs.

Carrie has always enjoyed a glass or two of wine when she comes home as it seems to help her relax whilst cooking supper. Recently she has found that she is drinking more than her usual two glasses and is often finishing the whole bottle before going to bed. Unfortunately, she now finds herself waking at 3 am, with a splitting headache and unable to get back to sleep. In the morning she feels heavy-headed and un-refreshed and starts the day feeling bad tempered and jaded.

When Carrie's husband suggests that she might be drinking more than is good for her Carrie angrily disagrees and says she feels that she is completely in control of her drinking. She welcomes the relaxation that she gains from it and basically feels that it is helping her to cope with the problems she is experiencing at work.

Carrie is adamant that she can stop drinking whenever she wishes. She is not (at this point) able or willing to see that her wine consumption is probably exacerbating an already difficult situation.

Although initially alleviating the symptoms of stress, and providing a 'feel good' factor, part of the physiological function of alcohol is to depress functioning on most levels. Hence performance goes down and, when sober, anxiety goes up.

Carrie has unwittingly placed herself in the classic trap of allowing an apparent solution to compound the original problem.

Individual reactions to stress can be easier to identify in some situations than others.

STEP 2
Gauging the Reaction

 Business is a combination of war and sport.

Andre Maurois

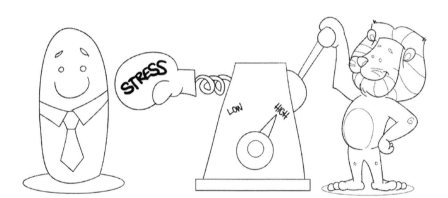

Discovering Why Stress is Different for Everyone

We may tend to think that everybody responds to pressure in the same way, but that is rarely so. The individual nature of stress means that we all manage the pressures that can give rise to stress in very different ways.

Whilst a modicum of pressure is necessary to ensure that we are kept motivated, excessive pressure can turn into stress that can adversely affect our everyday life, our health, our performance and our personal relationships.

When we are exposed to stressors, either in a social or working environment, we may react emotionally by becoming anxious or depressed, de-motivated, restless or possibly angry.

How we react to stressors will be influenced by our individual susceptibility to pressure, which in turn depends on our:

- Life experiences and conditioning
- State of health and beliefs
- Personality type
- Inherited genetic influences – our DNA

Other factors include our:

- Age and gender
- Religion, culture and race
- Income and level of education
- Family, social partnership and parental status
- Personal self esteem

Personal reactions to stress may be extreme and will usually affect our behaviour. We may start to overeat, or become withdrawn in an effort to seek release from tension.

We may find ourselves driving dangerously too fast, or being quick-tempered and irritable with our family, friends or colleagues.

Symptomatically, we may not recognise our own change of behaviour and may be likely to deny it when it is brought to our attention.

This is because it is usually not possible to see ourselves objectively - particularly when we are under excessive pressure.

> We are all susceptible to stress and are therefore vulnerable to its consequences. Although each of us has different levels of natural immunity and ability to cope, no one is entirely exempt.

the Nature of Stress

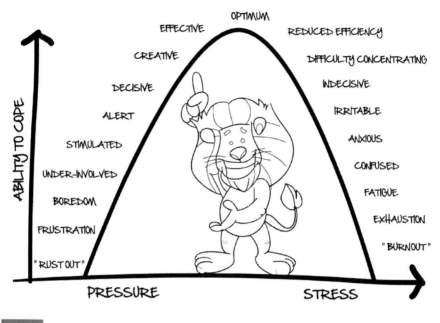

OPTIMUM

EFFECTIVE   REDUCED EFFICIENCY

CREATIVE   DIFFICULTY CONCENTRATING

DECISIVE   INDECISIVE

ALERT   IRRITABLE

STIMULATED   ANXIOUS

UNDER-INVOLVED   CONFUSED

BOREDOM   FATIGUE

FRUSTRATION   EXHAUSTION

"RUST OUT"   "BURNOUT"

ABILITY TO COPE

PRESSURE   STRESS

Fig. 3

Our vulnerability to stress can also be influenced by life events that may put us under emotional strain.

However, some people are more resilient than others as they have better coping resources and know when to seek support and/or guidance.

In the main, people often need to adapt their behaviour and learn coping skills in order to manage their stress levels. Relaxation, rest, exercise and a good diet all help to build natural resistance to stress and to boost our immune systems by lowering our reactions to stressful events.

The Relevance of Behaviour Types to Stress

Type 'A' and 'B' Behaviour

The questionnaire in Fig. 4 will help you to assess whether your usual behaviours are likely to make you more or less prone to stress.

Circle one number for each of the statements below which best reflects the way you behave in your everyday life. For example, if you are generally on time for appointments, for the first point you would circle a number between '7' and '11'. If you are usually casual about appointments you would circle one of the lower numbers between 1 and 5.

Casual about appointments	1 2 3 4 5 6 7 8 9 10 11	Never late
Not competitive	1 2 3 4 5 6 7 8 9 10 11	Very competitive
Good listener	1 2 3 4 5 6 7 8 9 10 11	Anticipates what others are going to say (nods, attempts to finish for them)
Never feels rushed (even under pressure)	1 2 3 4 5 6 7 8 9 10 11	Always rushed
Can wait patiently	1 2 3 4 5 6 7 8 9 10 11	Impatient while waiting

Takes things one at a time	1 2 3 4 5 6 7 8 9 10 11	Tries to do many things at once, thinks about what to do next
Slow deliberate talker	1 2 3 4 5 6 7 8 9 10 11	Emphatic in speech, fast and forceful
Cares about satisfying him/herself no matter what others may think	1 2 3 4 5 6 7 8 9 10 11	Wants good job recognised by others
Slow doing things	1 2 3 4 5 6 7 8 9 10 11	Fast (eating, walking)
Easy-going	1 2 3 4 5 6 7 8 9 10 11	Hard driving (pushing yourself and others)
Expresses feelings	1 2 3 4 5 6 7 8 9 10 11	Hides feelings
Many outside interests	1 2 3 4 5 6 7 8 9 10 11	Few outside interests
Unambitious	1 2 3 4 5 6 7 8 9 10 11	Ambitious
Casual	1 2 3 4 5 6 7 8 9 10 11	Eager to get things done

PLOT YOUR SCORE HERE	**TYPE B**		**TYPE A**
	14	84	154

Fig. 4 Source: Cooper's adaptation of the Bortner Type 'A' scale

Which Behaviour Type Are You?

Type 'A' and Type 'B' behaviour are personality types that identify those individuals that are likely to be stress prone.

The original research by Meyer Friedman and Ray Rosenman found that typically patients with coronary heart disease exhibited remarkably similar personalities and that by testing for these characteristics, susceptibility to coronary heart disease could be predicted.

Type 'A' individuals show the behavioural patterns and associated coping styles that cause them to have a high predisposition to suffer stress-related problems, whereas those showing Type 'B' characteristics are more likely to be able to cope with stress.

Fig. 4 uses the *Bortner Type 'A' scale*. After completion of the questionnaire calculate your score and then compare the results with the descriptions over the page.

Your actual score is on a continuum from extreme Type 'A' to extreme Type 'B.' A significant number of people will be near the centre and may exhibit both Type 'A' and Type 'B' traits.

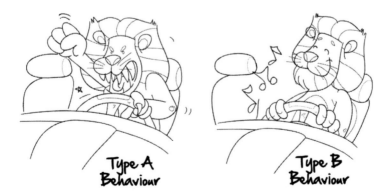

Type A Behaviour

Type B Behaviour

Scoring Results

Type 'A' is from score 84 to 154

Typical Type 'A' behaviours are likely to include impatience, aggression, ambition and competitiveness, and Type 'A' individuals are likely to be hard working, setting high standards and goals for both themselves and others.

They will have a great sense of time urgency, often setting unnecessary deadlines to drive themselves forward.

They will find it difficult to relax and are likely to have a feeling of guilt if they are taking 'time out' for themselves.

Evidence of these traits includes high levels of energy (including doing everything in a rush), often trying to do more than one thing at a time, completing sentences for other people and having explosive mannerisms such as table banging or shouting.

Type 'B' is from score 14 to 84

Typical Type 'B' behaviours are almost the reverse, i.e. not showing the above traits, but also Type 'B' individuals will be more in tune with themselves in that they feel no need to impress others with their achievements in order to gain personal satisfaction.

They will be much more able to relax and if they engage in physical activities they are likely to be in less competitive sports or will regard taking part as more important than winning.

They are much less likely to suffer from anticipatory emotions such as anxiety.

N.B. It is important to realise that this scale is non-judgemental.

It should not be taken as implying that the characteristics of either type are better, it merely indicates that people who have high Type 'A' are in greater need of stress awareness training and of developing coping skills.

People with high Type 'B' scores may wish to learn the skills of assertiveness and be aware that they might on occasions appear to be rather too laid back.

As in all personality indicators, one of the great advantages is that it helps us to understand and value the differences that we each bring to our work and our lives.

" *Watch your thoughts, for they become words.*
Watch your words, for they become actions.
Watch your actions, for they become habits.
Watch your habits, for they become character.
Watch your character, for it becomes
your destiny. **"**

Unknown

Exercise # 4

I Experience Type 'A' Behaviour When...

Think of a situation when you demonstrated Type 'A' Behaviour. What did you do? How could you have improved your management of the situation?

Situation 1

_____
_____
_____
_____
_____

What I do...

_____
_____
_____
_____
_____

What I could improve upon...

_____
_____
_____
_____
_____

Situation 2

_____

_____

_____

_____

What I do...

_____

_____

_____

_____

What I could improve upon...

_____

_____

_____

_____

_____

How to Move From 'A' to 'B' Personality Type

- Slow down and pace yourself
- Do one task at a time and really enjoy doing it!
- Use waiting time productively
- Try not to get angry over things you have no control over
- Try not to set yourself unrealistic deadlines
- Improve your time management
- Accept that mistakes can happen
- Enjoy participating in games – not just winning!
- Smile and show love and affection easily
- Practice listening attentively to others
- Learn to relax
- Open your eyes and appreciate nature and the environment

Some Advice for Those of Type 'B'

You may on occasion need to borrow some of the skills from your Type 'A' colleagues. This is especially so if you are a team leader or you are naturally unassertive. Remember to borrow these skills when and return to your less stressful Type 'B' philosophy.

Levels of Stress in Lifestyle Changes

Your experiences of having previously dealt with situations and people, whether adaptive or maladaptive, will also make a difference to how you react and cope with your future life events.

The loss of a close relation or life partner is acknowledged as being a very stressful event, whilst marriage and divorce also rate highly on the scale – albeit that marriage is ostensibly a happy event.

It is important to appreciate the common thread that links these events. In the vast majority of cases, it is the emotional impact of change that (fortunately) is usually short-lived and self-limiting. However, when we have a severe emotional reaction to an event or circumstance that is prolonged, this can then cause psychological or physiological problems.

Unfortunately, such reactions are by no means exceptional in today's often frenetic and pressurised lifestyle. In addition, economic, political and social stressors must also be taken into account.

These may include such factors as crime, increased violence, natural disasters such as flooding or epidemics, uncertainty, social isolation and media intrusion, together with the sheer pace of life in the 21st Century.

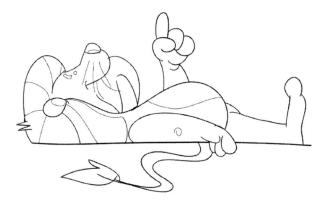

How many stressors are you trying to avoid?

In 1967, psychiatrists Thomas Holmes and Richard Rahe examined the medical records of over 5,000 medical patients as a way to determine whether stressful life events might cause illnesses.

Patients were asked to tally a list of 43 life events based on a relative score. A positive correlation was found between their life events and their illnesses.

Thus, the Social Readjustment Rating Scale (SRRS) or the Holmes and Rahe Stress Scale was born.

To put this into perspective, consideration needs to be given to the fact that this questionnaire is asking you to look back at your life events, making the data retrospective. Use Fig. 5 to check out how many stressors you have to manage in your life.

The aim of this exercise is to identify which of these events you have experienced lately. If your score is high, don't get worried about it, as the aim is to find out what is going on in your life and identify those stressors that you have no control over.

If you are experiencing many of these, try and balance your life with those stressors that you do have some control over, e.g. if you are going through a bereavement, try not to move house at the same time, or change job.

It is about trying to use the resources that you do have effectively.

Holmes-Rahe Life Changes Scale (1967)

Read through the list below and tick the lifestyle changes you have experienced in the last 12 months. Then total up the points and compare your score to those outlined below. The points indicate your likelihood of illness.

Do bear in mind, though, that whether an event is a source of stress or not depends on how you view it, and that your level of stress may relate to the number of the events you have recently experienced.

There are no right or wrong answers.

Death of a partner	100	Responsibility change	29
Divorce	73	Child leaves home	29
Separation from partner	65	In-law problems	29
Jail sentence or being institutionalised	63	Personal achievements realised	28
Death of close member of family	63	Partner starts or stops work	26
Illness or injury	53	Starting a new school	26
Marriage	50	Leaving school	26
Loss of job	47	Changes in living conditions	25
Reconciliation with partner	45	Changes in personal habit	24
Retirement	45	Trouble with employer	23
Health problem of family member	44	Change in working hours	20
Pregnancy	40	Change in residence	20
Sex problems	39	Change in recreation	19

Addition to family	39	Change in church/spiritual activities	19
Major changes at work	39	Change in social activities	18
Changes in financial status	39	Small mortgage taken out	17
Death of friend	37	Change in sleeping habits	16
Disagreements with partner/spouse	35	Family get-togethers	15
Change in line of work	36	Major change in eating patterns	15
Large mortgage taken out	31	Holiday	13
Mortgage or loan foreclosed	30	Christmas	12
		Minor violation of law	11

150-199 points increases your likelihood of illness by 40 per cent

200-299 points increases your likelihood of illness by 50 per cent

300 points and over increases your likelihood of illness by 80 per cent

Fig. 5 *Source: Holmes & Rahe (1967). Holmes-Rahe life changes scale. Journal of Psychosomatic Research, Vol. 11, pp. 213-218.*

The Importance of a Support Network

No matter how many of the above stressors have been affecting you, it is important to be aware that coping with stress can be made demonstrably easier with support from colleagues, family or friends. Strong and caring relationships are of primary benefit in helping you to learn how to cope with pressure and counteract stress.

'A problem shared is a problem halved' is a rather well-worn phrase, but in the area of stress management it is undeniably true.

Everyday Stress-Inducing Situations

In addition to major life events, there are also many situations during our normal day-to-day home and working lives which, depending on the circumstances, can act as sources of stress. The following examples are intended to demonstrate the types of situations that can result in stress and how they typically manifest themselves.

- You may have the inclination and belief that you have the resources to carry out a particular task, but in fact **the task may in reality exceed your ability to cope with it.** This mismatch in capacity may be due to adverse environmental factors such as excessive noise, heat or cold that can weaken your resolve or hinder your performance. In addition, resources that you thought you could rely on may not, in the event, actually be available to you.

- **Too high a self-expectation**, or the excessive demands that others may make upon you, can engender a need to prove yourself. Your subsequent inability to cope or to perform at the required standard can easily cause you stress.

- **Having inadequate internal resources** with which to meet a challenge, or too little control over a situation may also cause stress. You may be asked to complete a particular job but have insufficient skills or equipment to do so, thereby making the situation potentially stressful. However, once given the appropriate level of support, it is possible to view the situation or problem as a challenge that can be evaluated and met, thereby keeping you out of the 'stress zone'.

- You will almost certainly have experienced occasions when the anticipation of an unwelcome or embarrassing event has caused you great anxiety, but in reality the expected problem either did not materialise or the magnitude was less than expected.

  It is often the case that you **over-estimate the problem and under-estimate your resources.**

- Stress can also be caused by **the lack of opportunity to utilise your own ability effectively.**

  For example, someone may seek work to pay off a mortgage or loan and take a job that gives no satisfaction other than the monthly salary gained.

The experience of working daily with little or no job satisfaction may well induce feelings of frustration and anxiety that will eventually become stressful.

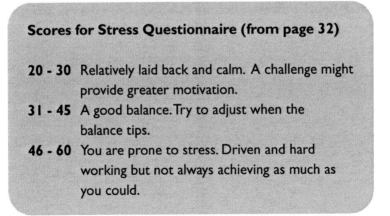

Scores for Stress Questionnaire (from page 32)

20 - 30 Relatively laid back and calm. A challenge might provide greater motivation.

31 - 45 A good balance. Try to adjust when the balance tips.

46 - 60 You are prone to stress. Driven and hard working but not always achieving as much as you could.

STEP 3
Getting to Grips

" Intolerance of groups is often, strangely enough, exhibited more strongly against small differences than fundamental ones. "

Sigmund Freud

Early Warning Signs of Stress in Your Team

Recognising and managing stress in your team is an essential managerial skill. An awareness of the individual strengths and weaknesses of team members, together with the ability to recognise when staff are under-performing or behaving unusually, is vital if stress is to be managed effectively.

Early recognition of frequent changes in mood and/or behaviour will enable appropriate support to be offered and performance to be reviewed before any serious health or safety issue arises.

Some of the Warning Signs

The following are just some of the warning signs that will give an indication that stress may be adversely affecting any one of your team:

1.   Increased unexplained absenteeism and minor sickness absences.

2.   Reduction in work performance, without any apparent reason.

3.   Tendency to lose concentration on the job in hand.

4.   Increase in workplace errors, accidents or 'near misses'.

5.   Change in timekeeping habits, for example persistent lateness.

6.   Working long hours without any apparent need (although this may be indicative of problems outside of work, i.e. that being at work is preferable to being at home).

7.   Seemingly withdrawn before and during meetings (possibly with frequent trips to the toilet) or failing to make any contribution to the subject under discussion.

8. Taking an irritable or aggressive stance with business associates, customers and/or suppliers.

9. Avoidance of face-to-face contact (e.g. emailing someone who is sitting in the next office).

10. Loss of ambition (e.g. failing to apply for promotion).

Remember, difficulties in people's lives outside work, may make them more vulnerable to workplace stresses.

Exercise # 5

Do You Recognise Any of These Signs of Stress in Your Team?

Poor timekeeping	Clock watching, leaving early
Reduction in output	Accident prone
Inclined to be forgetful	Poor judgement
Lack of personal care	Volatile and moody
Socially withdrawn	Poor decision making
Poor time management	Inability to meet deadlines
Low morale	Frequently absent
Erratic performance	Poor interaction with others
Reduced efficiency	Careless and sloppy

Common Causes of Work-Related Stress

There are of course many workplace stressors, but the following are the ones that feature in industry, time and time again.

Poor Management Style

The style and methodology with which management tackles day-to-day issues is clearly important in order to preclude them from becoming real problems. At all levels, there will usually be a pressure to perform in respect of workloads and targets. However, if this pressure is prolonged, it can be stressful.

Of course, the reality is that there is always the opportunity for stress to occur as a consequence of the power and authority that goes with a management position, no matter what management style exists within an organisation. Unfortunately there are managers who can be regarded as 'stress carriers' as they create rather than reduce the incidence of stress in their department. As we saw in the case study of Helen and Rema on page 47, in such situations it is not unknown for employees to look forward to those times when their managers are out of the office in order that they can get on with the job in hand.

It is therefore most important that the particular management style employed achieves the appropriate balance between consultation and control. In situations where work is delegated, adequate management training and support should be sufficient to pre-empt the emergence of problems that could well have been foreseen.

Just as an autocratic management style can alienate staff and create unnecessary workplace stress, so weak management can destroy motivation and morale and create an unseen pressure of lethargy and uncertainty. Both ends of the spectrum are unacceptable and both can lead to an unhealthy workplace culture and ultimately insidious bullying behaviour.

Workplace Bullying

Workplace bullying has been on the increase over the last few years in many industrialised and developing countries around the world. Every year in the UK, for example, millions of working days are lost to industry as a direct result of workplace bullying, costing the British economy billions of pounds and massively impacting on productivity, creativity, morale and general employee wellbeing.

Bullying behaviour may be confused with and viewed as:

- Personality clash
- Attitude problem
- Autocratic management
- Poor management style
- Harassment
- Abrasiveness
- Intimidation
- Unreasonable behaviour
- Victimisation

Being bullied is an isolating experience that tends not to be openly discussed in case this increases the risk of further ill-treatment. Those who are the prime targets often feel ashamed to discuss it with colleagues in case their professional credibility is called into question.

Employees who have experienced workplace bullying describe it in the following ways:

- 'This relationship is different to anything I've experienced before.'
- 'I'm persistently shouted at for no good reason.'
- 'My work is forever being criticised even though I know my standards haven't slipped.'
- 'I'm beginning to question my own ability.'
- 'I wonder if all these mistakes are really my own fault.'
- 'My supervisor is overbearing and constantly rude.'
- 'My boss is constantly ridiculing me in front of my team.'
- 'I don't want to go into work anymore. It's making me ill.'

Workplace bullying is a major stressor. Staff who experience bullying behaviour report lower levels of job satisfaction and higher levels of job-induced stress. They are more likely to be clinically anxious and depressed, experience low self esteem, and also to leave the organisation. Most will feel powerless to do anything about the situation, fearing that the bullying could get worse and they may well lose their job.

Case Study
Bullying at Work

Phil, a building society manager, had worked harmoniously with his team for eight years. Staff turnover in his department was low, and sickness levels were usually below average.

However, when Phil's Group Manager retired, the position was taken by Anna, a former colleague. What ensued was six months of extreme discomfort and harassment as Anna gradually eroded Phil's authority, ridiculed him in front of his staff and unreasonably increased his workload. When Phil sought help, Anna questioned his competence to lead a team and manage the branch.

Phil became very nervous, over-anxious, confused, and his health began to suffer. Anna's style of management was not person-centred, and her constant references to the need for staff changes in the branch resulted in Phil's anxiety turning to blind panic.

Anna's constant setting of unrealistic tasks was unremitting. The pressure she placed on Phil eventually resulted in him experiencing disturbed sleep patterns, chest pains and violent headaches. His deteriorating health, however, brought no sympathy from Anna. Even when stress was eventually diagnosed, she continued to undermine his authority. Phil was forced to conclude that he was the victim of psychological bullying over which he had no control. Unable to contain his anxiety and panic, he sought further medical help and finally broke down completely.

After nine months of sick leave, Phil was eventually forced to leave the building society. At his exit interview he unequivocally expressed his concerns about Anna. He believed that by highlighting the problem he had experienced, action would be taken to ensure that Anna's unacceptable behaviour would be curbed. His comments were regrettably not taken seriously by his employer, and no action was taken. This allowed Anna to continue in her uncommunicative and aggressive manner, which resulted in a further staff member leaving and another suffering a nervous breakdown.

Despite this catalogue of damning evidence that highlighted Anna's shortcomings as a manager, she still remains in a managerial post with the same employer!

Poor Communication Skills

Regrettably, there are managers who still believe that actively listening to their employees is a threat to their authority and weakens their ability to issue directives. Their fear is that by establishing a rapport with an individual they will blur the boundaries of an employer/employee relationship.

Active listening involves indicating that the speaker is being heard, and subsequently offering feedback. The manager who uses 'active listening' as a management tool will invariably generate an ethos of responsiveness, loyalty and co-operation from their team.

There are managers who tend to believe that managing people is solely and exclusively about work-related issues.

It is however most important to appreciate that individuals may have home-related problems to deal with, and that these can conceivably exacerbate work-related issues or vice-versa.

Managers should be proactive in communicating with their teams and need to appreciate that:

- An authoritarian attitude is not always appropriate

- The managerial skill of 'active listening' is an essential part of effective people management

- Obtaining optimum performance from their team is the duty and responsibility of every manager

Using bi-annual appraisals as the only contact time in which to talk directly to every team member on a one-to-one basis is totally inadequate, as is the practice of not allowing a two-way dialogue during an appraisal. Viewing the appraisal solely as a mandatory task to be carried out to a prescribed format reduces the chance for a quality dialogue between manager and employee. It also means that the benefits of exploring how members of the team are coping, or indeed whether they have any specific training needs to enable them carry out their duties, is effectively lost.

Many managers still believe that listening is a 'soft skill'. That it may be, but it is a soft skill with a hard edge attached!

Unrealistic Demands

Work overload and unrealistic demands are common causes of stress. As organisations shed staff, so those left behind find themselves under more pressure to achieve higher volumes of work and meet almost impossible targets. As well as asking more of employees, some organisations are offering less and less support.

With layers of management being removed in a bid to contain costs, employees are finding themselves reporting to more than one manager, carrying workloads that are often beyond their training and capability, and juggling deadlines that are often unrealistic.

When reviewing and revising demands on employees, it is important to ensure that:

- The organisation provides employees with adequate and achievable demands in relation to the agreed hours of work

- People's skills and abilities are matched to the job demands

- Jobs are designed to be within the capabilities of employees

- Employees' concerns about their work environment are addressed

Long Hours Culture

Maintaining a reasonable balance between work and home life is an increasing challenge for many employees. Contractually, a working week is often likely to be in the region of 40 hours. However, many of us will spend far longer than this thinking about our work out of office hours, taking work home with us, answering emails, and in some cases even taking work on holiday.

With an ever increasing number of different stresses emanating from home and from work, each may serve to exacerbate the other. Effective personal stress management is essential if we are to lessen the adverse impact of stress and improve our resilience, and thus our mental and physical health.

Today, much emphasis is placed on the importance of achieving a correct work-life balance and improving personal wellbeing. With the end of 'a job for life' – which was once a relative certainty in many economies, but is now increasingly rare - there is a tendency for work to take over our lives. As a result of this, more and more of us are living to work instead of working to live.

Employees are in some instances being made to feel guilty if they leave the office or workplace on time. Weekend working is becoming the norm for hard pressed executives - with many people finding it hard to take time off without feeling guilty.

Some organisations even inculcate this mindset in staff as the cultural norm. Clearly, by so doing, they impact on the external activities that employees would otherwise be able to undertake, thereby reducing the 'quality time' they could be spending with their families and friends.

'Presenteeism' is an unhealthy attitude adopted by stressed employees who remain at work when others have gone home. It frequently leads to individuals feeling guilty about taking their annual holiday entitlement, and for these employees it is often a case of 'don't forget your mobile phone and your laptop', rather than 'don't forget your passport and your sun screen'!

However, presenteeism can also be a symptom of home-related stress, when the employee prefers to be at work rather than at home. Some people choose to work long hours to avoid their partners or families, whilst others may work longer hours to make up for other inadequacies in their private lives. Whatever its cause, presenteeism is effectively the opposite of absenteeism and can be just as detrimental to business.

In many cases the erroneous belief is that such visibility improves the chances of keeping your job and of future promotion. However, the results of this behaviour are often high levels of stress, psychosomatic illness, depression and poor performance – adding (ironically) to the very risk of job loss that the employee is so anxious to avoid.

Case Study
Presenteeism

Marios, a solicitor, wears a suit to work but keeps an extra jacket on his chair at all times, so that Kamal, his director, cannot easily check on him to monitor when he is in or out of the office. It is not that he is not pulling his weight, but every day Kamal works a twelve-hour day, from 7 am to 7 pm – and Marios cannot keep up.

Q: Is Marios working effectively?

Q: Does working long hours improve Marios's productivity?

Q: Is Kamal setting the right example and getting the most out of his team member?

The answer to all the questions posed above is 'No'.

It may be the culture of the organisation to work these long hours, but the business must appreciate that just because an individual is at work and ostensibly behind his or her desk, this does not mean that they are being productive or working at optimum performance – often the contrary is true.

The extent to which long hours cause a problem for employees can also be influenced by the amount of control they have over their working time, with individuals who work long hours on a voluntary basis being less likely to be affected.

Most individuals can work at an excessive pace for a short period of time without adverse effect. However, when this pace is continuous, it can lead to ill-health and 'burnout'.

Case Study
Long Hours Culture

Harry, an experienced analyst, worked for a bank in the City of London.

His contract of employment and conditions of service clearly stated that his working hours were '9 am to 5 pm, Monday to Friday, with some overtime if required.'

A year into his contract Harry was working most evenings until 7 or 8 pm and taking work home every weekend.

One Monday morning, Harry's wife Kate phoned his boss to inform him that her husband had suffered a heart attack on Friday evening and was now in the Cardiac Care Unit of the local hospital.

She had been told that Harry was lucky to have survived and that although he should make a good recovery, he was likely to be off work for the next four months.

Kate wanted to know why Harry had been working such long hours. She had found his contract of employment and questioned why he was told his hours would be 9 am to 5 pm. She also sought legal advice.

Prior to this incident occurring, Kate was incensed that on two occasions in the previous year Harry had cancelled their holiday arrangements.

On the first occasion he had too much work to do and told Kate that he had to be available in the office to prepare vital reports.

On the second occasion, his holiday was cancelled at short notice when his boss told him that he had only just remembered he had booked three weeks' holiday himself and they could not both be out of the office at the same time.

" *I come to the office each morning and stay for long hours doing what has to be done to the best of my ability. And when you've done the best you can, you can't do any better.* **"**

Harry S Truman

With technological advances, new ways of working, and against a backdrop of job insecurity, employees certainly do feel the need to justify their existence in terms of the hours they are seen to be working – and hence their indispensability.

Case Study
Excessive Working Hours - Karoshi

'Nobuo Miuro, age 47 years old, was simply getting on with his job when he suddenly keeled over and died. It had been an extremely busy few weeks for the interior fitter from Tokyo; he had been struggling to get a new restaurant ready for its launch and had been putting in excessive overtime. The day before he collapsed he had worked from 11 a.m. to 4.30 a.m. the next morning, but had managed to snatch a few hours' sleep before starting again. However, when Miuro tried to pick up his hammer and nails again, he suddenly fell ill. He died a week later. The coroner returned a verdict of 'karoshi' – death by overwork. However, there are signs that some Japanese companies are introducing 'no overtime' days, meaning that for one day a week, workers get to actually go home when they have completed their contracted hours.' *(The Guardian, March 2001).*

'In January 1994, a junior doctor, Alan Massie collapsed and died in Warrington District Hospital at the end of an 86-hour week. He had worked seven of the previous eight days including two unbroken spells of 27 hours and one of 24 hours. The British Medical Council estimates that junior doctors frequently work more than 100 hours a week – equivalent to 16 hours 40 minutes a day for 6 days out of 7!' *(Observer, 10 April 1994).*

As the case studies illustrate, long hours do not necessarily equate to increased productivity or high levels of performance. Similarly, while working long hours may be viewed by employers as a way of obtaining the maximum benefit out of limited resources, in the longer term these effects are not sustainable, and have a negative impact on individuals and the organisations for which they work, and ultimately on the economy in general.

Exercise # 6

Of the following potential stressors, tick those that you think might be causes of work-related stress in your organisation.

The Working Environment

- ❏ Poor physical working conditions
- ❏ Insufficient personal space
- ❏ Lack of privacy
- ❏ Open plan office
- ❏ Cramped layout
- ❏ Uncomfortable room temperature
- ❏ Inadequate lighting
- ❏ Too much background noise
- ❏ No external windows

Tools for the Job

- ❏ Not suitable for the job or environment
- ❏ Out of date and/or in poor condition
- ❏ Unreliable / not looked after
- ❏ Regular / constant breakdowns
- ❏ Badly positioned
- ❏ Ergonomically unsuitable
- ❏ Add to noise and heat levels

Organisation Profile

- ❏ Insufficient staff for current workload
- ❏ Too many unfilled posts
- ❏ Poor communication between departments
- ❏ Insufficient training to fulfil the role
- ❏ Inadequate information given
- ❏ No control over workload

- ❏ Rigid working procedures
- ❏ No time given to adjust to changes

Interpersonal Relationships
- ❏ No opportunity for social interaction at work
- ❏ Sexism / sexual harassment
- ❏ No respect for diversity
- ❏ Conflicts with family demands
- ❏ Split loyalties between own needs and organisational demands
- ❏ Bullying culture

Organisational Management
- ❏ Inconsistent approach
- ❏ Emphasis on competitiveness
- ❏ Continual crisis management
- ❏ Internal power struggles
- ❏ Constant changes
- ❏ Overtime culture
- ❏ Shift work

Working Relationships
- ❏ Poor relations with the boss
- ❏ Unsatisfactory relationships with colleagues and subordinates
- ❏ Difficulties in delegating responsibility
- ❏ Personality conflicts
- ❏ Little or no feedback from colleagues or management

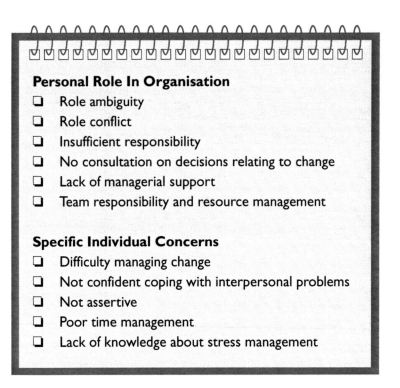

Personal Role In Organisation
- ❏ Role ambiguity
- ❏ Role conflict
- ❏ Insufficient responsibility
- ❏ No consultation on decisions relating to change
- ❏ Lack of managerial support
- ❏ Team responsibility and resource management

Specific Individual Concerns
- ❏ Difficulty managing change
- ❏ Not confident coping with interpersonal problems
- ❏ Not assertive
- ❏ Poor time management
- ❏ Lack of knowledge about stress management

Depending on your responses to the above, there are a number of steps you may or may not be able to take to help reduce stress in your working environment. For example, are there any simple changes you could make to your physical working conditions or the equipment being used? Are there issues that could be improved through discussion with your colleagues and/or superiors? Are there changes you need to make personally in order to reduce your vulnerability to work-related stress? Or are there issues that need to be tackled for the benefit of your team?

In this section we have looked at some of the telltale warning signs and most common causes of workplace stress. All can be regarded as components of an unhealthy workplace culture and are likely to contribute to high levels of absenteeism, reduced productivity and low morale in organisations where they remain unchecked. Our goal therefore has to be to reduce and ultimately eliminate the most frequent causes of stress and invest in a healthier working environment.

Proven Organisational Stress Management Initiatives

Bearing in mind the cost of stress in terms of lost production, lost sales and problems with staff retention, organisations are strongly advised to consider how they can best manage stress effectively.

Support in the form of coaching / counselling for employees who experience workplace stress will lessen the impact on the organisation as a whole and keep costs to a minimum.

The following initiatives will assist with this process:

1. Rationalise the Stress Management Function

Review the developing needs of the organisation and its workforce. Provide a business case for the phased provision of stress management training and support and routine risk assessment.

2. Strategy / Policy / Procedure

All organisations should have a policy for managing stress, designed for the protection of the employee and the employer. Policies should be constructive and not adversarial if they are to be effective.

3. Stress Awareness Training

Stress Awareness training for employees at all levels in the organisation is desirable with the aim of encouraging a supportive corporate culture and philosophy.

4. Stress Management Training

All those with a supervisory or management role should be given stress management training to assist them in recognising, managing and reducing stress levels in their staff.

5. Workplace Employee Counselling Support

Management training should ideally include listening / workplace counselling skills so that when managers are faced with having to assist their staff with work-related stress issues and/or personal problems they will feel more capable in doing so. Knowing how to approach an individual can be highly constructive and can produce a very effective response.

6. First Contact Support Teams

Consideration should be given to training volunteers in workplace counselling skills to help deal with employees' stress-related issues - providing boundaries, limitations and professional competence levels.

7. External Coaching / Counselling Services

Increasingly organisations are providing support for employees via telephone and face-to-face coaching / counselling services.

8. Stress Mediation

Providing neutral arbitration between management and employees is essential as preventative action is designed to avoid situations escalating out of control.

The Relationship Between Stress at Home and at Work

Whilst the pressures of work are often more than sufficient to result in us experiencing stress, the likelihood of this will be increased still further if we are also subject to excess pressures in other areas of our lives. We cannot realistically leave home, close our front doors and leave our personal problems behind - they inevitably will go to work with us and influence our behaviour in the workplace. The same is true with work-related problems. They will be in the back of our minds long after we have left the office no matter how hard we try to block them out.

Stress, whatever its cause, does have a detrimental effect on an employee's work performance and will make it difficult for them to withstand the ordinary pressures of work.

In Fig 6 on the next page, employees are exposed to a range of work-related stressors shown from the left, whilst home-based stressors are indicated from below.

Individuals will have the ability to cope with some of these pressures from either source and these are shown as being deflected by the employee.

The danger occurs when individuals are facing pressures that exceed their ability to cope and they then combine to increase the risk of stress-related injury and ill-health.

Providing stress awareness and coping skills training at work will benefit employees regardless of the cause of their stress.

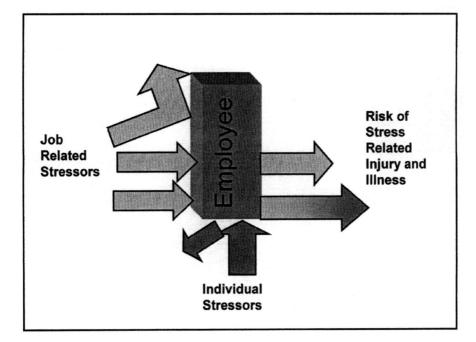

Job Related Stressors

Employee

Risk of Stress Related Injury and Illness

Individual Stressors

Fig. 6

Exercise # 7

What Causes You Stress at Home and at Work?

Write a list of those activities or situations that cause you stress, for instance, commuting, domestic arguments or speaking in public. Identify whether the stressor is from 'home' or 'work'. Now, complete this questionnaire and see the impact stress has on you both at home and at work. Many people erroneously believe that they can isolate stress problems by closing the front door of their homes as they leave for the office and vice versa, but sadly this is rarely the case.

Home	Work
←——————— Commuting ——→	
Domestic Arguments ——→	
←——————— Speaking In Public	

The challenge for all managers is to decide exactly how to set about recognising and identifying the causes of workplace stress, and more importantly, how to manage the problems they find. The **'HOW TO'** content of this book contains practical tools and advice to help you to do this. It has been created to provide you with valuable insights into the effective management of stress both at home and at work, and a toolbox of skills to call upon in the future.

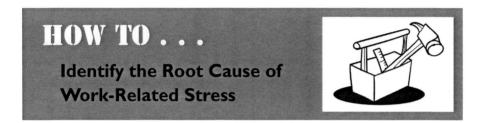

HOW TO . . .
Identify the Root Cause of Work-Related Stress

Sometimes employees will report that they are overloaded and are under more pressure than usual. In some cases the reasons will be apparent to them and they will not hesitate to tell you the cause. In other cases they might not be sure themselves. Even if they can identify the causes, they may be reluctant to disclose the real reason and offer a more general phrase such as 'my workload is really heavy'. These individuals could be reporting the first signs of stress. It may help to use the following checklist to see what has changed in their work that has triggered this extra pressure.

You can use this list of possible causes of stress to identify what has changed and what is causing the additional pressure. It is not anticipated that you go through this as a tick box exercise with the employee concerned, but use it more as an aide memoire so that you can cover a wide range of possibilities. Remember, this is a fact-finding exercise not a counselling interview. This tool should not be used with anyone who is already showing signs of being disturbed or stressed. It should not be used to discover and discuss feelings.

Once the problem has been identified, you can then move on to discuss whether the situation can be changed. Try to involve individuals in identifying the solution, using questions like, 'What would need to happen to improve this situation?' or 'What would you like to see changed?'

A Checklist for Identifying the Problem

What has changed?

Remember to use open questions – Why? When? Where? What? How? Who?

Additional tasks
- Where are new tasks coming from?
- Are they permanent, temporary or seasonal?
- Are requests coming from management or customers?

Change of responsibilities / staff shortages
- Are they temporary?
- Are they due to sickness absence?
- Are absences stress-related?
- Are existing staff working efficiently?
- Is equipment operating correctly?

Has the working environment changed?
- Has office location and/or layout changed?
- Are there problems with lighting, noise, cleaning etc?
- Have new managers been appointed?
- Are there new team members?
- Have shift patterns changed?
- Is there any confusion about individual roles/ responsibilities?
- Has there been a specific incident or accident?
- Are employees in overall good health?
- Have there been changes in employee's personal circumstances?
- Have employees received adequate induction/ skills training?

Self-Reported Stress

You may be uncertain as to what specific action you should take if members of your team report to you as being 'stressed'.

Firstly and most importantly, you should take their remarks seriously and allow time to address the issues raised. Remember, stress is an individual response to excess pressure and you may not be aware of how they actually feel.

It will almost certainly have taken some courage to admit to you, as their manager, that they are suffering from stress. By accepting what they say and dealing with them with understanding and empathy, you will help them to accept that stress is not a sign of weakness and that it is a normal human condition which we all face at some time or other in our lives.

The last thing that they would wish to hear are empty platitudes such as 'pull yourself together' or even worse 'other people can manage, so why can't you?'

We have already mentioned the importance of employer / employee communications and it is worth reinforcing here the difference between 'hearing' and 'listening'.

> What you think, say and do must always be congruent to the problem.

'Hearing' is a physical sense, and by itself makes you aware of the message. However, in order to understand the meaning of the message, there is a need for the intellectual skills that are called into play for 'active listening' to take place.

Remember! Your time is the greatest gift you can give to anyone.

Risk Assessment and Stress Audits

The Management of Health & Safety at Work Regulations (1999) make it a legal requirement for all UK organisations to assess the risk from stress and this is equally good practise for all organisations, wherever they are geographically located.

Risk assessment is a straightforward and logical procedure and can prove to be of positive benefit to both an organisation and its employees. By carrying out thorough risk assessments and planning the most suitable interventions that will effectively reduce or eliminate the problem(s), staff can be prevented from being adversely affected by stress. You will find all the information you need about stress risk assessment on the UK Health and Safety Executive website at: www.hse.gov.uk/stress.

As well as risk assessment, a stress audit is an effective method of identifying workplace stress issues and those employees who might be at risk. The audit involves talking informally to staff - either individually or in groups - to find out where there may be concerns about stress in the organisation. Essentially it is a research tool but not one that should be put in a drawer and forgotten! Once the results are published, an action plan is essential or the exercise becomes academic. All too often the action plan is left gathering dust and senior management lose credibility having raised employee expectations that they really do care about workplace stress and want to something about it.

Stress-Related Absences

If the early warning signs of stress are ignored by an employee and/or their manager, the end result will often be an extended period of absence from work – with all the attendant additional pressures upon the employee's team and colleagues.

The link between attendance and stress is so well proven that absence statistics are often used as an indicator of 'hot-spots' of stress within an organisation. The figures can also be used as a control to measure the effectiveness of any stress awareness interventions.

Attendance problems caused by stress fall into two main categories:

- The **long periods** of sickness absence of those already suffering from stress are immediately apparent and form a large part of the absence statistics in most organisations. Whilst it is too late to prevent the stress that has already made these employees ill, actions can be taken to actively manage their return to work to minimise the time away and at the same time reduce the risk of the stress recurring.

- It is however far more important to monitor the **short absences** that may be the first sign that excessive pressure is turning into stress. Typically, absences that fall into a pattern, such as every Monday, or ones that are linked to particular operational requirements such as reporting periods, are likely to be stress-related.

> Remember to look at the pattern of absence and not just at the declared reasons.

Stress is typically under-reported as a reason for absence, especially in the early stages, and reasons often given for odd days off are typically colds, back pain or headaches.

This under-reporting could be for several reasons: it may be that the individual has not recognised that they might be suffering from stress, or that they are reluctant to admit that this is the problem.

Successful intervention at the early stages of stress-related absences will create a culture that will enable staff to admit to stress-related ill-health problems without feeling that there is any stigma attached or that their future prospects are damaged.

The earlier the condition is diagnosed the sooner action can be taken. With early intervention it may be possible to avoid the excess pressure turning into stress and the associated long-term sick leave that often then ensues.

HOW TO . . .

Improve Your Management Style

Effective people management is a skill that many managers find difficult. It is however an essential skill if you are to lead your team with confidence and achieve consistently good results. The following tips will help you to develop a good rapport with your team and meet your common goals.

- Expect the best from people and you are likely to get it. Encourage a 'can do' culture in a realistic way. Encourage individuals to come up with ideas on how they may be better able to achieve targets, not reasons why they cannot.

- Facilitate feedback. Individuals appreciate the chance to say how they perceive both you, as their manager, and their job, and you may get valuable insight.

- Be approachable, listen whenever you get the opportunity and develop a reputation for being a 'good listener'.

- Reduce uncertainty to a minimum, and give employees information about whatever may affect their jobs, their environment or their future. Even if the news is bad, it is better to be open and honest rather than keeping employees in ignorance. At least with knowledge they can start to come to terms with the position and plan what actions they can take.

- Be watchful regarding hours of work, both your own and your staff. You cannot expect 100% performance for 14 hours a day, from anyone. Make sure everyone takes proper breaks away from the job - however brief.

- Encourage employees to make time for planning activities and improving relationships with others.

- Try to foster an atmosphere where you can all enjoy your work and one another's company.

- Think about team building opportunities and social meetings. Build relationships with your team, find out about their families and life outside work and any problems they may be experiencing.

- Ensure you and your team have regular, structured appraisal interviews.

- Don't hesitate to make a referral to a specialist, either internal or external, if you feel an employee is in need of advice and support that you are unable to provide.

Counsellor

❝ *My style will be management by being on the street, management by walking around. Third persons won't have to tell me what's going on in our city. I'll hear it, I'll see it, I'll touch it myself.* **❞**

Carl Stokes

HOW TO . . .

Improve Your Communication Skills

Our words can sometimes lose their resonance and our style and tone can offend. We assert when we should inform. We reject when we interject. We push people away when we should pull them in.

Effective business communication is often a neglected factor in management training – yet it is an essential component of the Manager's toolbox.

Good communication reduces the incidence of misunderstanding and consequent errors, and enables you to make your point quickly, clearly and persuasively. It also ensures that individual team members are more readily aligned to the vision and leadership of the organisation. This in turn serves to reduce the opportunity for disharmony, discontent or dissatisfaction in the workplace, and is supportive of a healthy working culture.

In the international arena, clear and concise communication improves understanding and helps with the accurate dissemination of information between you and your business partners, enabling both you and your team to work efficiently and effectively towards a positive outcome.

It goes without saying that effective communication also includes active listening skills, engaging with the person you are listening to and responding appropriately to them.

Employees may often choose to leave a company because of the poor interpersonal skills of a manager or supervisor. Not listening or understanding your employees' needs can result in dissatisfied employees who gladly turn to a competitor to fulfil their next need.

Effective communication enables managers to be more aware of the internal and external pressures on teams, and offers the opportunity for flexible and efficient management. Interviews, complex negotiating, conflict resolution, arbitration and mediation are just some of the many potentially difficult situations where the right word at the right time can truly 'save the day'.

Effective communication skills are skills for life! The way you communicate reflects the type of person you are. It gives an insight to your strengths and weaknesses and sets the tone for your business dealings. Poor communicators often make bad decisions, and worse still can be ineffective people managers and stress carriers.

If you are travelling on business or working remotely, you will be dependent on your central office to co-ordinate your activities. In this situation, the communications with your staff members will often be by email or telephone and, if these connections are poor, the integrity of your communications may be lost. It is in such scenarios as these that mixed or conflicting messages may be given or received, and it is therefore vital to ensure that conversations and instructions are confirmed in writing so that any ambiguity is avoided.

Email is a powerful tool that has taken over as the preferred mode of communication for busy managers, but it can also be problematical. In haste, you may well write exactly what you are thinking at that moment and hit the send button. However, it is always wise to reflect and re-read an email before sending, especially if you are, for some reason, frustrated or annoyed with the person to whom you are writing.

The Communication Skills Model

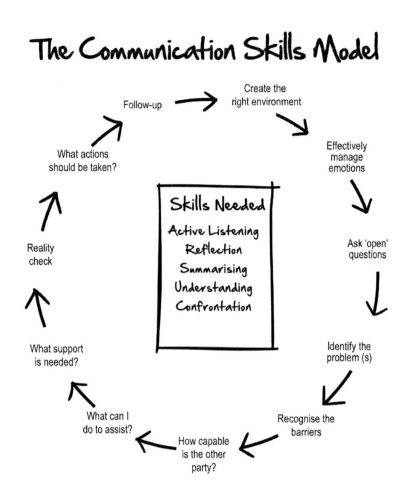

Listening skills

Listening is an invaluable communication skill and one that every successful manager needs to have. Whether you are dealing with organisational change, managing a redundancy situation such as breaking the news, or just dealing with day-to-day workplace situations, active listening plays an important role.

Listening is an art as well as a science. It does not necessarily come easily to all managers but it is important that it is mastered and forms part of every manager's toolbox of skills.

Anyone who is working under pressure, experiencing difficulty in cross-cultural communication or coping with personal problems may be less productive, short tempered and exhibiting poor time management. In consequence, their level of communication will often be below the standard required and the result can be reduced performance.

Employees may be reluctant to discuss their problems with you or anyone else in the organisation. They may, for example, see it as a question of their general ability to cope if they ask for help or feel that they are merely highlighting their own inadequacies.

'Active listening' is a particularly valuable listening skill. To find out more about how to develop your skills in this area, see page 117.

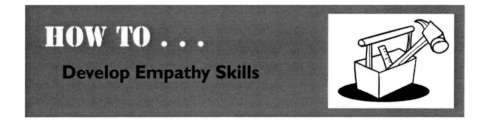

HOW TO . . .
Develop Empathy Skills

Showing Empathy

Empathy is a vital skill that as a manager you need to fully appreciate. It is only when you have true empathy that you can really understand what is being shared with you.

Empathy is therefore one of the most powerful communication skills we can use. It is a key skill when dealing with complaints, managing conflict and conducting successful negotiations.

❝ *Empathy is having one foot in someone else's world, but not both.* **❞**

Spiers C. Tolley's Managing Stress in the Workplace (2003)

To show empathy, we need to effectively reflect back the feelings the speaker is articulating. This important skill enables us to build an effective rapport even in difficult circumstances – with angry customers, negotiating partners, distressed employees – in fact, any circumstance that requires delicate handling.

The following techniques will help you develop your empathy skills:

- Practice reflecting back content with others – colleagues at work and/or family members. At home, try to reflect back to them what you think they have said (paraphrasing) and check out your understanding.

- Try to imagine someone you are helping in the various situations that they describe to you as if you were making a documentary video. Try to create as accurate a picture as you can on the screen of the experiences they describe.

- If you do not think visually, imagine the person as the key character in a novel you are reading or writing - think of all the phrases to describe this person and the situations they outline to you. It can be particularly helpful to think of yourself writing their biography.

- Work on increasing your vocabulary of emotions - use dictionaries, a thesaurus, novels, films and any other materials you can to enrich the way you can describe what a feeling is like.

- Be innovative - create your own exercises.

Empathy works because it demonstrates that we really are listening and understanding how the individual is feeling. Empathising enables us to show that we understand a person's feelings without actually agreeing with their point of view. It is therefore particularly important when attempting to deal diplomatically with conflict.

HOW TO . . .

Develop Active Listening Skills

Active listening is a remarkable way of responding that encourages others to continue speaking, while enabling you to be certain that you understand what they are saying. To use these skills effectively, you need to first grasp what happens when someone speaks with you.

Interpersonal communication begins intra-personally. Someone has a feeling or idea to express and in order to convey his message to you, he must first put the message into verbal and non-verbal codes that you will understand. The code he selects, the words, gestures and tone of voice he uses to convey his meaning, will be determined by his purpose, the situation and his relationship with you, as well as by such factors as his age, status, education, cultural background and emotional state. The process of translating mental ideas and feelings into messages is called 'encoding'.

How and When to Use Active Listening

Active listening is very useful in two specific situations:

1. When you are uncertain what the other person means
2. When an important or emotionally charged message is being sent

When you employ active listening skills, concentrate on reflecting the feelings others express, the content, or both - depending on what you think you might have misunderstood and what you consider most important. To arrive at your statement, ask yourself, 'How is he feeling? What message is he trying to convey?'

Active Listening Demonstrates your Acceptance

If you were to find yourself in each of these problem situations, which of these three responses do you feel would be the most helpful?

A child cuts her finger and begins to cry.

a.   'That's only a scratch.'
b.   'Stop crying! It really does not hurt that much!'
c.   **'Your finger looks like it really hurts a lot'.**

A close friend confides, 'My boss said I am not working fast enough and he will fire me if I don't get my act together.'

a.   'I guess you'd better make more effort.'
b.   'Don't let him wear you down. You can always get another job.'
c.   **'Sounds like your job means a lot to you and you would really not want to lose it.'**

The first two responses to each example tell others how they should feel or what they should do, or they express approval or disapproval, sympathy or reassurance. Responses like these seldom help or satisfy those who confide in you. Instead, they generally lead them to conclude that you don't want to get involved, that you don't take their feelings seriously, or that you have little faith in their ability to solve their own problems.

The third response, the *active listening* response, would have quite another result. Being encouraged to express their emotional reactions fully and freely helps others to become more relaxed and calm around you. Having their problems understood and reflected - but left with them - shows them that you have faith in their ability to arrive at their own solutions. Also, being heard, understood and accepted without criticism by you will inevitably lead others to feel more positive about themselves, warmer towards you, and more interested in hearing what you have to say.

Using Active Listening with Your Team

The use of active listening skills will help you create a team that is more open and forthcoming. Employees can sometimes be reluctant to speak to their managers – particularly in times of change or uncertainty when they may feel that any sign they are not coping may be held against them. In such situations, active listening is a particularly valuable skill, as it is a non-judgemental, facilitating process which enables you to:

- Value people for themselves
- Encourage individual growth
- Recognise someone's right to autonomy
- Avoid stereotypcal thinking, such as sexism, racism etc.

Active listening is a vital component of any interview situation but is especially important when undertaking:

- Return to work interviews
- Appraisal interviews
- Performance reviews
- Exit interviews

It is at times such as these that you need your toolbox of skills next to you. There may be unexpected situations to manage, unforeseen questions, and challenging behaviour to deal with. Your Listening Skills toolbox will see you through these times.

HOW TO . . .

Plan and Conduct Return to Work Interviews

Return to work interviews are an integral part of managing sickness absence and present an excellent opportunity to explore, on a one-to-one basis, the actual reasons for absence, and to offer employees support, where appropriate.

It may well be that absence is not actually caused through ill-health, but is merely a mechanism for taking time off to deal with pressing personal problems.

A 'listening ear' and some flexible management can possibly reduce the risk of unscheduled absence, and give employees the opportunity to take more responsibility for their attendance.

Return to Work Interview Plan

1. Plan the interview in advance at a mutually convenient time and place.
2. Conduct the interview in private, ensuring an atmosphere of confidentiality.
3. Set boundaries of confidentiality and agree a time frame.
4. Allow enough time for the employee to fully explain his/her situation.
5. Agree a return to work plan so that the employee is not overwhelmed with work. This is especially important when the employee is returning from a period of long-term absence.
6. Make a written record of the interview for future reference.

Where it is apparent that there is an ongoing health problem, there may be the opportunity for the organisation to offer support to employees, either via an Occupational Health department or through private medical care.

To 'listen' you need sound but to 'hear' you need interest.

HOW TO . . .

Conduct an Appraisal Interview

Appraisal interviews present an ideal opportunity for employees to discuss their concerns about their work and for managers to evaluate performance.

1. Appraisal interviews should start and end with a positive comment with any negative issues being sandwiched in between. Remember to encourage employees to talk, use listening skills so they can see you are genuinely interested, and encourage participation in any decisions such as setting goals or objectives.

2. Use listening skills and try to understand their point of view and give them support. Don't be abusive or exploit them. Try to be fair and discrimination will not be a problem. Always be seen to value what employees do. Individuals should know exactly what their job consists of and have a written job description. Delegation should be done clearly with employees knowing what is expected of them on a daily basis, when you want tasks completed by, and how much you wish to be kept informed of their progress.

3. Give regular objectives, preferably in writing, three-monthly, six-monthly or yearly. Employees should have a part in deciding what they are and the objectives should be reviewed regularly.

4. Be assertive, and honest with yourself and with others. Tell an employee face-to-face if they do something that annoys you, but take issue with what they did rather than make it a personal attack. Being passive and saying nothing may result in an eventual aggressive response when you cannot continue to hide your feelings.

5. Praise individuals when they deserve it. You may want to ask yourself if you have a moral right to complain about performance if you fail to mention when they do well.

6. Consult over deadlines and targets where you can and endeavour to make them realistic, wherever possible.

7. Make sure the working environment is appropriate and try to avoid giving boring or repetitive work on a continuous basis.

8. Try to behave calmly yourself, don't rush about, speak slowly and try not to become annoyed and unnecessarily irritable.

9. Be aware of the importance of confidentiality in your dealings with employees and also of the limits of confidentiality.

10. If you are presented with a problem that may be beyond your own skills and resources to deal with, make sure you know where to refer to obtain help.

> Value each person's contribution. Reward is not just about financial remuneration. Recognition can be just as important as money.

HOW TO . . .

Conduct Exit Interviews

By the time an employee has decided to leave the company, it is probably too late to change their minds. However, valuable information about the culture of an organisation can be gleaned from an exit interview.

There is much learning to be gained from exit interviews as employees usually have little to lose by giving their feedback. The interview should be a friendly, two-way conversation with the use of 'open' questions to give the departing employee the opportunity to 'offload'. It should not be intimidating in any way.

Here are some examples of questions that can be used at exit interviews:

- What is your main reason for leaving?

- What could have been done early on to prevent the situation developing and provide a basis for you to stay with us?

- What specific suggestions would you have for how the organisation could manage this situation and / or these issues better in future?

- How do you feel about the organisation in the light of your experience?

- What has been good / enjoyable / satisfying for you in your time with us?

- What has been frustrating / difficult / upsetting to you in your time with the company?

- Did you ever experience any bullying or intimidation on grounds of religion, gender, nationality or ethnic group?

- How would you describe the culture or 'feel' of the organisation?

- How well do you think the appraisal system worked for you?

- What would you say about how you were motivated, and could that have been improved?

- What can you say about the way you were managed? On a day-to-day and month-to-month basis?

- How could the organisation reduce stress levels among employees where stress is perceived as an issue?

- What things did the organisation or management do to make your job more difficult / frustrating / non-productive?

- How can the organisation gather and make better use of the views and experience of its employees?

- What do you feel the organisation can do to retain its best people (and not lose any more like you)?

- Would you consider working for us again if the situation were right?

- What is your new employer offering you that we are not?

Confidentiality is all-important when conducting an exit interview, and it is desirable that there is trust on both sides so that the information provided can be used in a constructive way.

The interview should be conducted in private and reassurances given that disclosures about colleagues will not be directly referred to in any subsequent actions.

HOW TO . . .
Know 'What To Say' and 'What Not to Say' in a One-to-One Interview

One-to-one sessions with employees who may be stressed at work and/or have personal problems are never easy. Here are some examples of what you really should <u>not</u> say in a one-to-one meeting. These are judgemental words and offering opinions, and do not encourage talking an issue through.

'WHAT <u>NOT</u> TO SAY'

'I think you should/ought/must ...'

'You have got to snap out of it...'

'It's not important, it really doesn't matter ...'

'Clearly...'

'Never...'

'Are you sure?...'

'Everything will be alright...'

'Don't you think you are blowing things out of all proportion ...'

'The problem is ...'

'Let me give you some advice ...'

'It's pretty clear what you should do...'

'I know exactly how you feel ...'

'I understand how you feel ...'

'You obviously won't want to ...'

'You obviously are/feel ...'

'Why don't you ...'

'That's not much of a problem ...'

'Didn't you know that ...'

'Can't you see ...'

'Don't be silly ...'

'It could be worse ...'

'I don't believe it ...'

'The best thing for you is ...'

'What I would do ... '

'Really, Gosh, Heavens ...'

'I know just the answer ...'

'Go away and forget it ...'

'What you have to do is ....'

'If I were you ...'

'You think you've got problems ... well ...'

'That happens to many people ...'

'I don't believe that ...'

'You must have felt ...'

'Come on, think of the positive side ...'

'There are many people who are worse off than you ...'

SEXUAL HARASSMENT

'Are you sure you're not imagining it ...'

'I can't believe John would behave like that ...'

'I'm sure he didn't mean it ...'

'Are you sure you are not encouraging him ...'

'Why are you telling me? ...'

'Pull yourself together ...'

'You are being silly ...'

'You don't really mean it ...'

'Don't think like that ...'

'Don't feel like that ...'

'You must be ...'

BEREVEAMENT

'You will get over it!'

'We all have to die sometime'

'It happens to all of us'

SOMEONE WHO FEELS SUICIDAL

'You don't really mean it'

'We all feel bad at certain times'

'Things will get better'

The following words and phrases give options of possibility and not opinions. They are empowering words and encourage people to think through their problems themselves and come to their own solutions. They are non-threatening and non-judgmental.

'WHAT TO SAY'

'It seems that ...'

'It seems as though ...'

'You also said ...Could you tell me what you mean by that?'

'Let me/can I check this out?'

'What would happen if?'

'Let's develop that a little further?'

'I was wondering whether?'

'It could be?'

'It may be ...'

'You said that (summarise) ... I was wondering if you could tell me what you mean by that?'

'It occurs to me ...'

'Tell me more about ...'

'How do you feel?'

'How do you feel about ...'

'I was wondering if I have got this right?'

'You seem sad/hurt/down ...'

'It could be helpful/useful' ...

'Could you explore/explain a little more of ...'

'It may be helpful to think about what we have said...'

In basic terms, clear and concise communication reduces pressure and improves understanding. It helps with the accurate dissemination of information throughout the organisation, enabling both management and staff to work efficiently.

It enables managers to be more aware of the internal and external pressures on their staff, and offers the opportunity for flexible and efficient management.

It can also enable the provision of suitable interventions in potentially sensitive situations such as instances of stress brought about by sickness absence, care issues or bereavement.

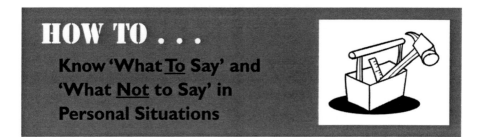

HOW TO . . .
Know 'What <u>To</u> Say' and 'What <u>Not</u> to Say' in Personal Situations

The following are some extreme examples of how not to address an employee, together with more acceptable alternatives. Unlikely as this may seem, they reflect the kind of language that managers can find themselves using when they themselves are under pressure – but this does not make them any more acceptable in a progressive workplace environment.

'Get this done now'
'Please could you give this job priority'

'Stop being so stupid'
'I'm not sure that you are tackling this problem in quite the right way'

'I don't care how you think you should do this job - I want it done this way'
'I think if you try the approach I'm suggesting, you'll achieve some good results'

'Keep quiet and go to my office now'
'Can you please come to my office so that we can discuss this'

'Stop behaving in such a ridiculous way'
'I'm sorry but I don't think your behaviour is appropriate'

'Not another day off! I guess it will have to wait until Monday'
'I know you are not in the office tomorrow so can you see me on Monday'

'Is this task too much for you? The trouble with you is that you can't stand the pace'

'I hope you're comfortable with this task but please let me know if you need any support'

'Not now. Come back later.'

'Can you please come back in five minutes?'

'I thought I told you to get this job done before your break. Do you ever listen to what I say?'

'Was there a reason why you were unable to get this done before your break?'

'If you want to get on in this company, you'll have to come in early and stay late'

'While we certainly look for commitment from our employees, it's important that work doesn't completely take over your life'

'I understand you were sick again yesterday!'

'I'm sorry you were not well yesterday. Are you OK now?'

STEP 4
Regaining Control

" *The pessimist sees difficulty in every opportunity. The optimist sees opportunity in every difficulty.* **"**

Winston Churchill

Pressure, Stress and You

Many people in executive positions experience stress at some point in their lives. You may find yourself challenged by work, relationships and domestic responsibilities, and you may feel unable to seek help and support.

In this section, you will find a variety of techniques that you can use to help you manage your personal stress levels and prevent them from developing into more serious problems. No single method works well for everyone, so it is necessary to find an appropriate technique which works best for you.

In the main, the positive actions you can take can be considered under three headings:

> **1: Changing behaviour**
>
> **2: Developing a healthy lifestyle**
>
> **3: Changing your mindset**

Even something as simple as positive thinking (although it may not seem that simple at the time!) will go a long way towards effective stress management.

All of us prefer to be among people who are lively, interesting and positive, rather than tired-out, negative and boring. How we are perceived by others is important for our own self-image, but when stressed, this can be easily forgotten.

There may be times when it is necessary to seek professional help, guidance or support. Where this is the case, it should not be seen as a sign of failure or weakness.

On the contrary, it is a sign of strength to be able to recognise our body's warning signs and to take appropriate action. Only in that way, can each of us ensure the continuation of good health, and retain control of our lives.

It is important to create an environment where stress-related issues can be acknowledged, discussed and properly addressed at an early stage.

These points are just as relevant to your working environment as they are to your personal life, and you should be aware that these considerations are as applicable to your staff as they are to you.

It is often the case that those very individuals who are the most vehement in denying that they have a problem with stress are the ones who are most in need of help, and it requires a trusting relationship to be established for these issues to be dealt with properly.

Once some success has been achieved in dealing with a particular aspect of stress, it is recommended that the method by which this was accomplished is remembered together with the learning that comes from it.

When future events in life overtax your coping resources, you will hopefully be able to then draw, with advantage, upon previous experience.

No. 1. Changing Behaviour

Changing the way you behave and interact with others can reduce pressure and ultimately help you to manage stress more effectively.

Proactive interventions to help you manage pressure better and avoid stress include the following:

- Keeping a stress diary

- Being more assertive

- Improving your time management

- Managing email effectively in order to save time

- Managing 'Type A' behaviour in yourself and others

- Benefiting from humour and laughter

- Reducing travel stress

- Utilising external help

HOW TO . . .
Keep a Stress Diary

If you find yourself in a situation where you are feeling under stress, it follows that it may well be both beneficial and instructive to keep a diary for 2-3 weeks, to help identify the reasons for the feelings you are experiencing that are related to excessive pressure.

Although for many people, the act of keeping a diary may itself appear to be an additional chore, it can prove invaluable in helping to understand not only the primary sources of your stress, but also the frequency with which you experience the effects of them upon your daily life.

Suggested Diary Contents

- It is better to keep the diary entries as brief as possible, provided that all relevant details of the impact of the stress experienced are included - such as any other persons involved, events, activities, time and duration.

- Details should include everything that puts a strain on available resources of energy or time which result in the physical, emotional or behavioural responses that we discussed earlier in the book.

- After a couple of weeks, the diary entries should be reviewed to identify the most important situational stressors that have affected you, in order that you can determine how best to deal with them effectively in the future. To retain a sense of proportion, you should also note the positive events in your life – those that are invigorating, pleasurable or which give you a sense of achievement.

Exercise # 8

Stress Diary Template

Day/Time	Situation	Physical Response	Emotions

Exercise # 8

Typical Stress Diary Entries

Day/Time	Situation	Physical Response	Emotions
Monday 6 September, 10.30am	Weekly meeting. Asked to comment on IT proposal.	Heart started to beat faster, hands became clammy and my voice sounded high.	Really anxious. Apprehensive that my comments would be considered inadequate.
Wednesday 8 September, midday	Took client to lunch.	Felt hot and uncomfortable. Hands shaky – spilled the water.	Nervous and embarrassed. Couldn't find the right words in order to maintain the conversation.
Thursday 9 September, 9.00am	Required to work in outer office, which was overly hot as air conditioning wasn't working properly.	Office so stifling I could barely concentrate. Only achieved half my planned workload. Ended the day tired and exhausted.	Became extremely irritable and bad-tempered. Shouted at Mona who came in to take a letter and who misheard what I had dictated.

Day/Time	Situation	Physical Response	Emotions
Wednesday 15 September, 4.15pm	I am told that I have to give my report in tomorrow morning instead of Friday.	Tried not to show how I was feeling, but my shoulders tensed-up and, later in the afternoon, I started to get a pounding headache. Found it really difficult to concentrate.	Annoyed and resentful at having to work on the report. Nervous because I didn't know if I could finish it on time.

Mauger S. (Spiers C. Tolley's Managing Stress in the Workplace (2003))

When situations such as those described have been identified as stressful, it is important to ask the following questions:

- Were these events or activities for me or someone else's benefit?

- Did I have any control over them or did they ostensibly control me?

- Was the handling of these situations really beyond the scope of my inherent or learned abilities?

Dependent on the answers to these questions, the next step is to try to alter the overall characteristics of your activities from being 'stress producing' to 'stress reducing'.

Actually removing or replacing people, events or activities that are causing you stress is rarely practical or feasible.

However, what you **can** do is to think about ways of reducing their negative impact and implementing positive interventions to bring about a better result and overall life balance.

It has been suggested that the addition of more daily 'pleasurable events' has more positive effect on the immune system than reducing stressful or negative effects – implying that small daily improvements can help transform a negative, stressful existence into a more positive and productive one.

Writing your feelings down on paper can also be an effective way of 'unloading' frustration and taking the heat out of difficult situations.

In the following sections, we will look in detail at a wide range of proactive interventions – starting with how you can try to change your usual behaviour and responses to stress.

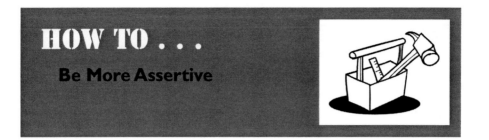

HOW TO . . .

Be More Assertive

Many people find it extremely difficult to say 'no'. They put themselves in invidious situations by accepting additional work or tasks when they have, in reality, insufficient time to complete them. The consequences are often disappointment in themselves and others that invariably leads to both physical and psychological stress, and a reinforcement of a poor self-image and reduced self esteem.

People can exhibit four distinctly different types of behaviour – **aggressive, indirectly aggressive, passive and assertive** – and for people who find it difficult to say 'no', assertiveness and time management training can both be extremely valuable.

Being Assertive **Is** About Being Able to	It is **Not** About
Hear what others say	Getting angry
Verbalise what you feel and need	Being aggressive
Negotiate	Selfishness
Reach an acceptable compromise	Being superior to others
Respect others	Always trying to get your own way
Be confident in all that you say and do	Being intransigent

Being recognised as non-assertive can allow others to 'walk all over you', because you effectively surrender control to them.

By comparison, being assertive equates to standing up for your personal rights, and expressing your thoughts, feelings, wishes and beliefs directly, honestly and spontaneously in ways that are not detrimental to the rights of others.

Assertive people take responsibility for their actions and choices, and even in cases of failure, notwithstanding the obvious disappointment, their self confidence and self respect will remain intact.

The expressing of negative feelings, at the appropriate time, also avoids the build-up of resentment – thereby helping assertive people to manage their stress more successfully.

It is important to note that it is not possible for a non-assertive person to change overnight. It takes time, practice and commitment.

If you find it difficult to say 'no', then serious consideration should be given to attending a training course on assertiveness - either trainer-led or by distance learning – and there are also some excellent reference books available on the subject.

If you frequently find yourself acting aggressively by shouting, being intimidating and generally making others frightened by your anger, you might also consider anger management coaching.

Aggressive behaviour not only alienates other people but, if persistent, can also seriously damage your health by releasing too much adrenaline into the body with the consequent impact on blood pressure.

It's Really OK to say 'No'...

To be able to say 'no' to unrealistic demands from work colleagues, or supervisors, is not the easiest decision to make when your job is of the utmost importance to you and the security of your family. It is even more difficult when there is often someone else who will invariably say 'yes' in order to improve their own position within the hierarchy of the department or the promotion list.

It is important to better understand why we invariably find it so difficult to say 'no' and often push ourselves beyond our personal limits of physical or mental capacity. Such disregard for our own welfare can result in serious work stress that can impair our personal performance either temporarily, or, in extreme cases, permanently.

Instances of mental breakdown, or burnout, when we find ourselves unable to cope with even simple requests, are, unfortunately, on the increase within our often harshly competitive corporate environment.

Very often we have grown up in circumstances where we are expected to be compliant, particularly to demands from those in authority over us - notwithstanding that those demands can sometimes be unduly onerous or even invalid.

This has led to an attitude whereby we perceive that to refuse a request or demand will lead to:

- A 'blot on our copybook'
- A hindrance to our promotion
- Our having a perceived inability to cope
- Our being seen as a person who is not a committed team player
- Appearing to be one whose priority is always ourselves and not our employer or organisation
- Our being seen as rude or un-cooperative

How and When to say 'No'

What is the correct way, therefore, to reasonably reject excessive demands at work?

The answer is in creating a culture of respect in which to decline an unreasonable request will be seen not as a mark of weakness but rather a position of strength. Where to seek an alternative way to achieve the necessary result without compromising personal wellbeing is the norm rather than the exception.

Those with high self esteem find it easier to say 'no' than those with low self regard. The latter often attempt to seek praise and affirmation from colleagues and will invariably always agree to any request. This is notwithstanding the harm it can do by compromising their health and wellbeing.

Saying 'no' can actually boost our self-esteem. It obviates resentment about being forced into situations that are unreasonable, and dissipates personal stress by feeling that we are in command of our own welfare.

Saying 'no' is an essential tool that everyone should be able to use within the appropriate circumstances. But in a highly competitive world, think carefully before declining a demand that may be entirely reasonable, and always:

- Give your reasons clearly and concisely, when refusing a demand
- Suggest alternatives that are reasonable and positive
- Avoid surrendering control by saying 'yes' under pressure.

You have a duty to protect yourself against burnout. Saying 'no' to excessive demands in the workplace requires determination and strength of character. However, to decline or refuse a request or demand that is not unreasonable would be imprudent indeed, and could jeopardise an individual's position or even career. Therefore, saying 'no' must be used judiciously.

" *Assertiveness is not what you do, it's who you are!* **"**

Shakti Gawain

The 'Positive – Negative – Positive' Sandwich Tool

One technique that you may find useful when you really have no alternative other than to say 'no' is the Positive – Negative – Positive Sandwich Tool.

Imagine a work situation where a colleague has asked you to do something which, for whatever reason, you simply cannot do.

Rather than saying 'yes' and creating a problem for yourself, or saying 'no' and leaving your colleague dissatisfied, the Positive – Negative – Positive Sandwich enables you to say 'no' in such a way that your colleague ends the exchange still feeling positive about you.

For example, in response to a colleague saying 'Can you complete this report for me?', try structuring your reply as follows:

- 'As much as I would like to do this…' – (shows your understanding.)
- 'Unfortunately I can't because…' – (stating a fact and a reason why not.)
- 'But what I can do is…' – (showing your willingness to help.)

The key is always to end up with a 'positive' statement, as this is the last thing the person will remember.

8 Simple Techniques to be More Assertive

1. Acknowledge your own feelings to yourself. If, for example, you feel angry, it can be helpful to acknowledge the feeling even if you decide not to express it.

2. Be clear about how you feel and what you actually want.

3. Be clear and direct in what you say. Misunderstandings often happen as a result of unclear messages.

4. Adopt a sound inner dialogue. What are your real thoughts about the situation you are currently facing?

5. If necessary, keep repeating your message. Often people are not really listening to what you are saying and may introduce something irrelevant into the conversation. Try repeating your message in order to receive some acknowledgement that it has been heard.

6. Use appropriate body language to back up your assertive behaviour. Adopt an open, relaxed posture with the head erect, and face the other party square on. Establish eye contact, and keep your voice steady and firm.

7. Keep calm and stick to the point. Relaxation exercises, such as deep breathing, can help.

8. Respect the rights of the other person. In some situations (as with negotiation), compromise is a preferable outcome.

Exercise # 9

Become More Assertive

I could be more assertive if I did not...

_____

_____

_____

_____

_____

I could be more assertive if I tried to...

_____

_____

_____

_____

_____

I know I will be more assertive when I have more
confidence in myself...

_____

_____

_____

_____

_____

_____

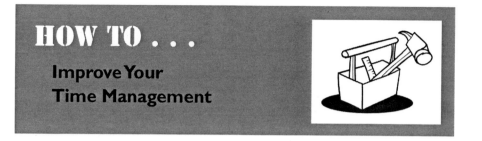

HOW TO . . .

Improve Your Time Management

How your time is managed is a key factor in determining the level of stress in your life. Many individuals complain bitterly that they are always short of time, but this can often be caused by:

- A lack of assertiveness
- Being unable, or apprehensive about delegating tasks to others
- Having an excessive workload
- Allowing time to be wasted – or not using time productively
- Prioritising jobs and tasks incorrectly

By comparison, good time management is about:

- Establishing priorities
- Making a list of what MUST be done, SHOULD be done, and if possible, what the person would LIKE to be able to do
- Eliminating time-wasting activities
- Getting into the habit of focusing on essentials
- Learning to say 'no' and being able to delegate effectively
- 'Chunking' your time into two hourly sessions to manage in-depth, creative tasks.
- Scheduling daily (uninterruptible) time to organise daily activity
- Not making excuses for <u>not</u> doing something
- Making a list of achievable goals or targets

One of the most difficult aspects of time management is assessing goals to determine whether or not they are achievable. For example, are the goals that you are trying to achieve realistic in the time available, and are they, in fact, what is really needed? This is sometimes difficult to ascertain and quantify, because individual goals can often be subsumed within the general needs of the organisation. This is why it is important to identify short-term, medium-term and long-term goals, and list tasks accordingly.

It may even be that someone else is actually responsible for the problems you are experiencing with time management, in which case you may need to work together in order to take remedial action.

It is also important to spend less time for fire fighting and set aside time for forward planning and team building. Try not to get too caught up with trivia and excessive distractions e.g. social networking, internet surfing etc.

> Set up precise targets. Make to-do lists and manage yourself by objectives.

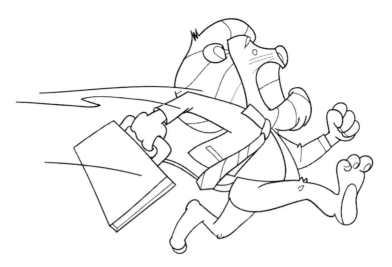

" *Time is a universal currency so stop racing through life at 150 mph or you will miss the good things in life...* **"**

'Asking for Time'

'Asking for Time' is about considering yourself and valuing your time. You need to remember your right to say 'no', as there is little point in giving yourself the space to reflect on your priorities if you are still unable to say 'no' at the end of it.

Before accepting any increase in workload, you may need to discuss any difficulties that this might entail, in order to negotiate a solution that is satisfactory to both yourself, the person or the organisation that is making the request or demand of you.

Essentially, the best way forward is to ask for time to evaluate the request or new instruction, in order to come to a decision that takes account of the effects of acceptance.

Priorities should be evaluated together with the consequences of refusing – as highlighted previously in the section on saying 'no'.

5 Easy to Use Time Management Strategies

1. Listen carefully to the details of a request and make notes if appropriate
2. If necessary, seek clarification to make absolutely sure of what is being asked of you
3. Confirm your understanding of the details of the request or instruction
4. Where necessary, seek time to consider the request
5. Confirm the amount of time you will need for the task and agree the mode of communication i.e. verbally, by email etc.

" *There cannot be a stressful crisis next week.*
My schedule is already full. **"**

Henry Kissinger

HOW TO . . .

Manage Email Effectively and Save Time!

Email was meant to make our lives easier, but many people have ended up feeling stressed out by their inboxes. Thanks to email, mobile phones and text messaging, we're expected to be on call 24/7 – even when we're out of the country. So all of us need the skills to manage emails more efficiently, before our stress levels increase even further.

The ideal would be to tackle email overload at its source – by preventing emails from arriving in the first place. Most email programs have filters to separate 'spam' emails from the ones we actually want, but can still direct emails to the wrong mailbox. It's important therefore to check your junk mailbox as regularly as your inbox, and make sure that 'junk' emails really are unsolicited mail before deleting them - otherwise you'll end up simply adding to your problems.

Wherever you work, you'll be familiar with colleagues who seem to feel the need to copy you in on every email they send – whether or not they are relevant to you. Added to which, there are the times when you signed up on-line for a purchase or subscription and you were required to give your email address. The result of which subsequently fills up your inbox every day with unwanted mail and then needs clearing.

Research suggests that many people are starting work earlier and earlier, simply to deal with the emails that confront them every day, and there are many stories of people who come into work an hour earlier and work an extra hour at the end of each day – just to catch up.

If this is happening to you, these **12 simple rules** will help you 'control the inrushing tide'. You need to manage your email the same way as you manage your time, as being organised is the key to 'good email management'.

1. Turn off your alerts and set yourself specific times to read your emails as it can be very distracting when you hear that 'ping' from your machine. You tend to respond immediately and break away from what you were doing to just read the message. Then it is more difficult to return to your task after this break in concentration.

2. Return unwanted emails – only then will the sender realise you didn't want them. Don't do this with unsolicited email though, as this can confirm to the sender that your address is 'active'.

3. Don't open email attachments from people you don't know – they may contain viruses.

4. Structure your mailbox – use folders to keep your messages well organised.

5. Have boxes for urgent, non-urgent and nice to read, so that when you need a break away from your day-to-day working, you have your reading email box waiting for you.

6. Be careful to flag up everything you have read. It's very easy to read an email and think you have responded when you haven't. This can be a problem if the recipient asks if you have given a response and you think you have when you haven't!

7. Before sending an email, select the best medium for your message. Is email the most appropriate communication and do you really need to send one? Many people have stopped phoning or walking round the office to see colleagues and would rather email them.

8. Make the purpose of your email clear. Put as much detail as possible in the subject line to help the recipient.

9. Use short words and sentences, and check your attachments before sending – many are unnecessary and could just as easily be included in the message itself.

10. Show consideration to the recipient by allowing time for responses. Expecting one immediately is unreasonable.

11. Never send an email when you're tired or angry.

12. Always check the addressee(s) and don't just copy everyone. You can cause considerable upset by emailing the wrong person!

Your company may or may not have an email policy, but this needs to be the responsibility of each and every individual. Be responsible for each email that you send out. Do all recipients need to be aware of the information you are sending them? Do they need to be copied in on this email?

Email is a wonderful tool but it needs to be managed. Keep in control of it – rather than it being in control of you!

HOW TO . . .

Manage Type 'A' Behaviour in Yourself and Others

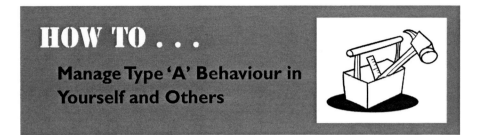

Many people like to blame any outburst or over-reaction they might exhibit on their 'Type A' personalities – an issue that is best explained through a case study.

Case Study
Managing Type 'A' Behaviour

'It's the way I am and the way I think – I have to be like this to get things done,' says Mary, the Sales Manager of a UK property company. 'It's because I'm a perfectionist and proactive that I get impatient with others who are less motivated.

There is also little doubt that I do not suffer fools gladly. If my staff had the same mindset and worked to my standards, there wouldn't be any problems and I wouldn't get so frustrated and angry. I know I am effective at what I do, and in my mind, the problem is with everyone else - there is definitely nothing wrong with me.'

Comment: *Mary is not helping herself, because she is fighting with her own personality to achieve and maintain control. She cannot accept the differences in others – who, from her perspective, are either doing the job her way or are doing it wrong. She also generates unnecessary stress for herself and for those around her* *with continuous and often unnecessary criticism, as a result of which her own stress response is being continually triggered. As a consequence of this negative behaviour, it is likely that one day Mary will simply break down or 'burnout'.*

This will occur as a result of her body having to cope with the continuous production of stress hormones that, in time, will impact and weaken her cardiovascular system. In order for Mary to improve her life expectancy, she would be well advised to adopt some of the following fundamental techniques for better personal control.

Wherever possible, reduce the demands made upon you by assigning tasks to others. Delegate to people whom you trust, ensuring that they are given clear, concise instructions regarding the job required.

Accept that delegation is the right approach in this instance, and then move on with your own work.

Checking at designated times can give a feeling of confidence to individuals, and will ensure that they feel supported, but not hounded. Constructive feedback is useful, but continual criticism is destructive and unhelpful.

Remember that the achieved result (and time taken) will probably be absolutely acceptable notwithstanding the fact that the employee is doing the job in their own way, which may be different from your chosen method of doing things.

13 Techniques for Managing Type 'A' Behaviour

I.   Avoid trying to be perfect

Accept the fact that you haven't failed just because you may not have completed a job perfectly. Accept that you have done your best, and try to stop being obsessive about getting everything right, 100% of the time. Human beings are fallible.

2.   Take your time

Always allow an extra 15 minutes to ensure you have time for yourself and also to clarify your thoughts and actions.

3.   Deal with one task at a time and enjoy what you do

Take your time as opposed to rushing through everything. After completing a task, sit back and reflect on what you have achieved. Has any learning come from it? Did you have problems meeting your deadline because you left some issues to the last minute? Utilise any learned experience to draw upon the next time you meet a similar situation.

4.   Use your waiting time productively

If you are waiting at the bank; for a train or at the checkout, then use this 'dead time' productively by planning or thinking instead of becoming frustrated about a situation over which you have no control.

5.   Try not getting angry over things that you cannot influence or change

Accept that there are some issues over which you have little or no control. When you have tried every possible way to achieve what you want, but without success, it may well be time to move on.

Becoming frustrated and angry about matters over which you have no control is pointless. Rational thinking should prevail over emotional reactions if you wish to maintain good health.

6. Acknowledge your mistakes and those of others

We all make mistakes, but we do not necessarily have to be punished for them. Ask yourself, 'Has anyone actually suffered loss as a result of this error?' Learn to accept with humour when something goes wrong and look to learn from the situation. It can often be instructive to listen to the details of someone else's mistake, and to think about what you would have done in similar circumstances.

7. Avoid sending angry responses to incoming email

Do not respond immediately to an email that has had the effect of provoking an emotional response, such as anger in you. Always take time to reflect, rather than reply immediately with an emotional response. Remember, that once the 'send' key has been hit, it is impossible to retrieve a message written in haste.

8. Enjoy competition without necessarily winning

Being competitive is fine, but not at the expense of enjoying yourself. Do your best and in so doing, you will maximise both your enjoyment and the pursuit.

9. Smile and give positive words of encouragement

Many managers walk into the office and rarely take the time to smile or say 'Good morning'. A personal greeting costs nothing and will make both colleagues and your team feel valued.

10. Praise and give thanks

Being able to give praise and positive feedback, and not just criticism, will enhance any relationship. Saying 'thank you' for a job well done costs nothing and means so much!

11. Take time to relax

It is essential to schedule relaxation time into your day for yourself. Set yourself realistic relaxation goals and try to keep to them.

12. Try to turn stressful life events into challenges for your own personal growth

Stand back and reflect. Commit to paper the learning gained from experiences so that the knowledge obtained can be turned to full advantage in the future.

13. Learn to be a good listener

Do not finish sentences for others, as apart from being discourteous, you cannot necessarily know exactly what they are going to say. Constantly interrupting and never waiting for a response will simply mean you will be regarded as a poor listener. People will be reluctant to share their thoughts with you if you do not listen, as there would be little point in doing so.

Learn to pose basic, open questions – 'what, why, when, who, how, where', in order to elicit a meaningful and interesting reply.

Listen carefully to what is said and follow the subject through. Keep an open mind and you will gain far more from conversations!

Now sit back and read a most wonderful heartfelt story that captures the very essence of 'listening'.

Once upon a time ...

A young and successful executive was travelling down a neighbourhood street, going a bit too fast in his new Jaguar.

He was watching for kids darting out from between parked cars and slowed down when he thought he saw something. As his car passed, no children appeared. Instead, a brick smashed into the Jaguar's side door. He slammed on the brakes and backed the car up to the spot from where the brick had been thrown.

The angry driver then jumped out of the car, grabbed the nearest kid and pushed him up against a parked car shouting, 'What was that all about and who are you? Just what the heck are you doing? That's a new car and that brick you threw is going to cost a lot of money. Why did you do it?'

The young boy was apologetic. 'Please, mister. Please. I'm sorry but I didn't know what else to do,' he pleaded. 'I threw the brick because no one else would stop...'

With tears dripping down his face and off his chin, the youth pointed to a spot just around a parked car. 'It's my brother,' he said. 'He rolled off the curb and fell out of his wheelchair and I can't lift him up.'

Now sobbing, the boy asked the stunned executive, 'Would you please help me get him back into his wheelchair? He's hurt and he's too heavy for me.'

Moved beyond words, the driver tried to swallow the rapidly swelling lump in his throat. He hurriedly lifted the handicapped boy back into the wheelchair, then took out a linen handkerchief and dabbed at the fresh scrapes and cuts. A quick look told him everything was going to be okay.

'Thank you and may God bless you,' the grateful child told the stranger. Too shaken for words, the man simply watched the boy push his wheelchair-bound brother down the road toward their home.

It was a long, slow walk back to the Jaguar. The damage was very noticeable, but the driver never bothered to repair the dented side door. He kept the dent there to remind him of this message: 'Don't go through life so fast that someone has to throw a brick at you to get your attention!'

Sometimes when we don't have time to listen, it may be necessary for someone to take extreme measures in order to gain our attention – especially when that person has no other voice with which to speak.

HOW TO . . .
Benefit from Humour and Laughter

In 1979, the American, Norman Cousins, then editor of the *Saturday Review*, published a book *"Anatomy of an illness as perceived by the patient: Reflections on healing and regeneration"*. The book describes his experience of the effects of humour on a severe illness (ankylosing spondylitis) which he contracted in 1964.

Deciding that the hospital regime of strong medication, unimaginative food and the institutional system were too depressing for any real benefits to be gained, he developed his own recovery programme comprising a mix of vitamin C and regular doses of laughter stimulated by re-runs of Marx Brothers films and 'Candid Camera'.

The treatment appeared to relieve his pain considerably, and indeed, when his levels of inflammation were tested, they were found to have dramatically reduced.

According to members of the Association for Applied and Therapeutic Humour, the psychological benefits of humour are quite amazing.

People often store negative emotions such as anger, sadness and fear, rather than expressing them. Laughter provides a way for these emotions to be harmlessly released, and laughing with someone can be an equalising experience that can defuse many a tense or awkward situation.

Humour gives us a different perspective on our problems. If we can make light of a situation then it becomes less threatening. Humour is a wonderful stress reducer and antidote to bad temper and tension. It is known that laughing relaxes tense muscles, speeds more oxygen into our system and lowers blood pressure.

It is also believed that laughter reduces the levels of certain stress hormones that tend to weaken the immune system. Laughter potentiates the ability of defensive cells to destroy tumours and viruses, as does gamma-interferon (a disease-fighting protein), T-cells (which are a major part of the immune response) and B-cells (which make disease-destroying antibodies).

Overall, the advice is to try to surround yourself with people who are able to make you laugh and help you to feel good about yourself.

HOW TO . . .

Reduce Travel Stress

Travel and commuting can be major stressors in our modern world.

The following techniques may help you to minimise travel stress:

- Always leave an extra 30 minutes to allow for inevitable traffic delays in order to ensure that you are on time for your meeting. If your journey does happen to run on time and you arrive early, then you will have space to think and relax before your appointment.

- Try not to make 'back-to-back' appointments, as meetings will frequently run over time and then you will be late and become stressed. It is always advantageous to have a short break in between appointments in order to collect one's thoughts and composure.

- Check your route before you leave, especially if you are travelling to an unfamiliar area, and if possible talk to others who make the journey on a regular basis.

- Make sure your car has sufficient fuel the day before your journey, and if necessary check tyres, oil, etc, rather than leaving this until just before you set out.

- Never drive immediately after an emotional upset such as receiving details of a bereavement or being involved in an argument, as your mindset and feelings might increase your risk of an accident.

- Have small change available in the car for parking meters, and carry a copy of your motor insurance certificate in the glove compartment in case you are involved in an accident or stopped by the police.

- Before starting out, adopt a comfortable seating position and adjust your seat and driving mirrors.

- On long journeys, remember to take short breaks to help avoid becoming over-tired. Keep your arms slightly bent and in a '10 to 2' position on the steering wheel for optimum control and to avoid fatigue.

- Whilst stationary or sitting in heavy traffic, try to perform simple relaxation techniques to help reduce tension in the body - especially vulnerable areas such as the neck, shoulders and arms.

- Have music in the car which you enjoy listening to so that you can use your time effectively. View your car as a personal time and space capsule away from everyone else - an environment which provides your own selection of music and radio channels.

5 Quick Commuting Tips

Travelling, by its very nature, takes place in a spatial context that is outside your control. You can be travelling down Oxford Street in central London or Sheikh Zayed Road in Dubai – it doesn't really matter which country you are in, traffic is traffic the world over!

1. Be tolerant of others - shouting at other drivers after what has clearly been their mistake will not change anything, but your anger will affect your judgement for some time afterwards. Remember that the other driver does not know you – bad driving by other road users is not a personal attack. The personalities of some people change when they get behind a wheel, and a calm Type B personality can become a supercharged 'Type A' rally driver as soon as they sit in their car.

2. Continual clock watching will not help you get to your destination any quicker, but will increase your stress levels and you will arrive more stressed than when you set out - and certainly not in a fit state to conduct yourself effectively at a business meeting. In fact, when you are late for an appointment, it may even be beneficial to physically cover up the clock in your car so that you cannot actually see the minutes tick by!

3. Accept that drivers (including you) make honest mistakes and have occasional lapses in concentration.

4. Be courteous and thank others for their courtesy. How many times do you become aggrieved because you let another driver out into a stream of traffic and don't even get a 'thank you' wave from them?

5. It can be advantageous, following a near accident, to re-examine the incident in your mind to ascertain what action could have been taken to avoid or pre-empt its occurence.

HOW TO . . .

Utilise External Help

There are occasions when you may be under undue pressure at home or at work, and at times like this external help and support can be beneficial. The following are just some of the many sources of help available.

Mentoring / Coaching / Counselling

As the proverb says, 'a problem shared is a problem halved'. However, there are occasions when friends or family, however supportive, may not be the people you feel you can turn to. You may feel embarrassed about discussing your worries - particularly if they are intimate. You may also be worried about confidentiality - not wanting the entire world to know about your problems.

In the workplace, individuals may also have a need for someone with whom to discuss problems, but they can be wary about talking to just anyone, in case they are perceived to be weak or unable to cope. They therefore may turn to a professional mentor / counsellor for confidential help.

There are many sources of support for specific personal problems such as bereavement. However, if you chose to select an independent coach or counsellor, it is advisable to ensure that they are active members of a professional body and are able to assist you with your specific issues.

The key factor is to find the right person with whom you feel comfortable. Just because one of your friend's recommends someone, it does not necessarily mean that they are right for you. Counselling is about the intimate sharing of thoughts and feelings and so who you choose is very important. It is a process to which you need to be committed as it provides a different perspective, although it takes time. If you think that it will improve matters overnight, then you will be disappointed. However, the personal awareness and learning that comes out of these sessions can be immeasurable, and the response and behavioural changes that you may make as a result will provide a greater insight into your response and behaviour.

Counsellor

Strengthening or Establishing a Support Network

It is recognised that a majority of those individuals who appear to remain happy, healthy and are able to withstand multiple life stressors, have the advantage of possessing a good network of social support – usually comprised of family and close friends.

In addition, professional support from outside sources such as The Samaritans, (a UK-based charity that operates a 24-hour telephone helpline for people in crisis and needing support) can also be extremely helpful. There are likely to be times when you might rather speak to a stranger than a friend. Confiding in a stranger who knows absolutely nothing about you and has no expectations of you enables feelings to be expressed within a safe framework.

When people with problems want to move on, they are often keen to draw a line under the issue that has caused them pain. They may no longer wish to discuss the difficulties they have experienced and are likely to be keen to look forward rather than back to unhappy times.

Whichever means you choose, it is important to be able to express your feelings with someone you trust. However, this does not necessarily have to involve an actual person. Venting feelings by writing a diary, or perhaps a letter that might never be posted, may have the desired effect of releasing and/or expanding thoughts and feelings.

Be aware however that no matter how much time and effort you put into changing your behaviour, you are unlikely to enjoy the maximum benefit unless you also ensure that you look after your body (and mind) through the development of a healthier lifestyle.

No. 2. Developing a Healthy Lifestyle

As you will see in this section, there are many different elements involved in the development of a healthier lifestyle.

Many people who embark on this process are often shocked to find out how unhealthy they really are. So, to introduce you to just some of the elements that are typically associated with living a 'healthy' life, you should answer the questions in the following lifestyle checklist as truthfully as possible.

It is a sad fact that given the pressures of modern living, many people will answer 'yes' to maybe just one or two of these questions.

If this applies to you, you should at least console yourself that you have already taken the first positive step in addressing the situation, and use this as a motivator towards becoming a better, healthier you.

" *It's never too late to mend your ways!* **"**

Exercise # 10

Now check out your score here and see how healthy you are!

Do You:

Do You:	Yes	No
Eat 5 pieces of fruit / vegetables per day?		
Drink less than 2 cups of coffee per day?		
Drink at least 2 litres of water per day?		
Walk at least 20 minutes per day?		
Know how to switch off and relax?		
Sleep well at night?		
Make time for hobbies?		
Make time for family and friends?		
Enjoy your environment?		
Make time for 'you'?		
Include fun and laughter in your life?		
Have regular breaks during your day?		
Put some 'me time' in your diary each day?		
Ask for help when you need it?		
TOTAL		

When you have completed the checklist (as truthfully as possible!), count up the relative numbers of 'yes's and 'no's. In an ideal world, we would all have 14 'yes's, but if you have more than seven 'no's, your first goal should be to improve the balance in your life by turning at least some of these into 'yes's.

To achieve this, start by looking at the 'no's that you think will be easiest, most pleasurable or least challenging to address, and use this as a tool to make positive changes to your lifestyle. You could also include a commitment to these changes in your Stress Diary (see page 139) to give yourself a constant reminder of the changes you need to make.

Mastering the capacity to rebalance your life by developing a healthier lifestyle is essential to help maintain the health of mind and body. An effective balance includes:

- Eating a healthy diet
- Improving your fitness
- Exercising at work
- Taking time out
- Achieving quality relaxation
- Getting sufficient uninterrupted sleep
- Improving your leisure time

" Life can be pulled by goals just as surely as it can be pushed by drives... "

Viktor Frankl

HOW TO . . .

Achieve a Healthy Diet

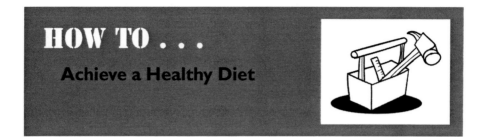

Our bodies are remarkably efficient at extracting the nutrients we need, but at times of stress, these needs increase and a well balanced diet is, therefore, essential in preserving health.

You may think you are eating well, but how many times do you just grab something quickly 'on the run' because there are not enough hours in a day?

How many times do you come home late in the evening and are too tired to eat properly? It is all too easy to get into bad habits, and those habits need to be broken if you are to remain fit, healthy and stress free.

It is very important to eat a balanced diet. In periods of intense pressure, eat food that is high in Vitamin B (wholemeal bread, whole grains, pasta and jacket potatoes) and Vitamin C (fresh fruit and vegetables).

Ensure you also have adequate amounts of green, yellow and orange vegetables which are all rich in minerals, vitamins and phytochemicals that are essential to boost immune response and protect against disease.

A healthy diet needs to be balanced to match your physique and lifestyle.

Carbohydrates

Complex carbohydrates such as rice, pasta, potatoes and bread result in a slow release of energy, which is important in maintaining a constant blood sugar level - particularly so for diabetics – as opposed to the 'quick fix' provided by sugar.

Carbohydrates also trigger the release of the powerful neurotransmitter serotonin that has an important role in the maintenance of mood control.

Fats

Fat is an important source of energy, but avoid the consumption of foods rich in animal (saturated) fats that cause obesity and increase cholesterol levels. Both these factors adversely impact the cardiovascular system and are a contributing factor in coronary heart disease (CHD).

Diets made up of a large proportion of processed foods are often omega-3 deficient which can contribute to bouts of depression. Foods such as coldwater fish, flaxseed oil and walnuts will help redress this balance and reduce the risk of mental health problems associated with stress.

Protein

Protein is responsible for repairs to skin, muscles and bones. It can be found in nuts, dairy products, meat and some beans and grains. There are two types of protein. Animal products supply complete protein and some plants supply proteins regarded as incomplete. For the body to get the amino acids it needs, it is necessary to combine protein.

Fibre

Fruits, vegetables and grains are excellent sources of fibre. These bulking agents are important for a healthy digestive system and it is recommended that a normal diet should include at least 25 grams of fibre per day.

Vitamins

Essentially, your body needs a range of vitamins to grow and develop. Vitamin C is especially important to strengthen your body's defence system, especially in winter. All the vitamins the body needs can be obtained from eating fresh fruits and vegetables or from vitamin supplements.

Minerals

Minerals help to build strong bones, create hormones and regulate your heartbeat. Fruit, vegetables and fish contain the minerals which are necessary to help release energy from food and improve brain functioning. This in turn can help you think more clearly especially during periods of stress.

Water

Water is essential to maintain life and for our bodies to operate efficiently, especially in very hot environments.

This includes temperature regulation, nerve impulse conduction, circulation, metabolism, the immune system, eliminative processes, sensory awareness and perceptive thinking.

Many people drink too little water. One glassful a day is not enough, as the many chemical processes inside the body require more than this for optimal completion of reactions.

It only takes a 1% fluid loss for the body to become dehydrated, and an insufficiency of water can seriously disrupt the body's biochemistry. This generally happens without any conscious sensation of being thirsty.

Stress and caffeine can both influence the amount of water available to the body's systems and the speed with which the body loses it.

Any of these factors alone, or in combination, may cause small but critical changes in the brain that can impair neuromuscular coordination, decrease concentration and slow down the thought processes.

The average amount of water loss per day is equivalent to two cups through breathing, two cups through invisible perspiration, and six cups through urination and bowel movements.

This equates to a total of ten lost cups per day that need replacing - without taking into account perspiration from exercise or hard work, air conditioning or caffeine consumption.

Furthermore, travelling by air can entail a loss of as much as one litre of water during a three to four hour flight. It is hardly surprising, therefore, that the daily recommended intake of water is 1.5 to 2 litres. When working in an air conditioned office or in very hot weather, your intake should be even more.

CAUTION: Health Warning.
Eat and drink the following with care!

Sugar

Sugar has no essential nutrients and it
provides a short-term boost of energy to the
body, resulting in excess fat deposits. High
sugar consumption over time can lead to
overweight, glucose intolerance and,
eventually, type 2 diabetes.

Salt

The consumption of 'convenience' foods
should be kept to a minimum, as most contain
either large amounts of sugar, salt, fat and/or preservatives. Salt increases
blood pressure, affects the adrenal gland and causes dehydration, thirst and
possible emotional instability. Sufferers from stress should use a low salt
substitute that has potassium rather than sodium, and avoid junk foods high
in salt such as ham, pickles, sausages, burgers etc.

Alcohol

When taken in moderation, alcohol has been shown to benefit the
cardiovascular system. Many people, however, take alcohol to combat stress,
but in fact by doing so make matters worse. Alcohol is a depressant, and
excess alcohol increases fat deposits in the body and decreases the immune
function. It also reduces the ability of the liver, over a period of time, to
remove toxins from the body.

When experiencing stress, the body produces several toxins which, in the
absence of efficient filtering, remain in the body as potential causes of damage.

Consuming large amounts of alcohol neither solves problems nor improves health. It is not a good idea to concentrate alcohol intake into just the weekend either! It is important to remember the recommended safe levels of alcohol per week are 21 units for males and 14 units for females (a unit is equal to just one normal size glass of wine).

Caffeine

Limit caffeine intake, as it is known to 'kick start' the stress reaction. Caffeine is found in coffee, tea, chocolate, cola drinks and some headache remedies. When taken in moderation, caffeine can increase alertness.

However, consuming an excess of caffeine – whether in coffee or cola – can be addictive and lead to irritability, sleeplessness and impatience.

Caffeine also acts as a diuretic, an excess of which can lead to dehydration. It is recommended to reduce coffee and caffeine consumption slowly over a period of time, as stopping abruptly can result in withdrawal symptoms.

HOW TO . . .

Improve Your Fitness

Exercise not only improves your general fitness and increases overall strength, stamina and suppleness, but it also has many other additional benefits. Self esteem can be raised and sleep patterns can improve – meaning that exercise is usually good for both the body and the mind.

The key benefits of exercise can be summarised as follows:

- Exercise improves cardiovascular function by strengthening the heart, causing greater elasticity of the blood vessels, increasing oxygen throughout the body, and lowering the blood levels of harmful fats such as cholesterol and triglycerides.

- Exercise provides a physical outlet for negative emotions such as frustration, anger and irritability, thereby promoting a more positive mood and outlook.

● Exercise improves mood by producing positive biochemical changes in the body and brain, as well as reducing the amount of 'fight or flight' hormones the body releases in response to stress. The body also releases greater amounts of endorphins during exercise - the powerful, pain-relieving, mood-elevating chemicals in the brain, which are often lacking in people who are depressed.

● Exercise is also an excellent distraction from stressful events and circumstances, and it is thought that stress itself poses significantly less danger to the overall health of people who are physically fit. This is because their heart and circulation are able to work harder for longer periods, and being physically stronger, they are less susceptible to musculoskeletal injury.

Exercise will therefore keep the body functioning properly; help you to feel relaxed and refreshed; promote deep, restful sleep and is a good stress management technique, because it:

- Reduces muscle tension and uses up the adrenaline and energy released by the 'fight or flight' response
- Makes the body stronger and better able to cope with the debilitating effects of stress
- Increases energy and stamina
- Maintains self image, appearance, and tends to control weight
- Helps to clear the mind of worrying thoughts

Feeling fit increases the overall feeling of wellbeing, and a commitment to exercise will increase feelings of control and self respect. If you are considering regular exercise, the following points are important to consider:

- Physical exercise is an excellent way of getting the necessary relief and increasing your coping resources – but you will need to make time for it.
- The choice of exercise is yours. Do something that suits you and fits in easily with your daily life.
- Begin with an exercise that you enjoy. Find a regime that is interesting, challenging and satisfying, and one that preferably also brings you into contact with other people.
- 20 games of squash or 15 aerobic workouts are unnecessary and can even be dangerous.

It takes as little as three 20-minute sessions per week to increase your physical fitness, and it will also stimulate mental acuity and help to combat the adverse effects of stress.

It is, however, recommended that if you are not used to exercising and are over 35, you should visit your doctor prior to embarking on any exercise programme in order to check that it is suitable for you.

The value of exercise cannot be over-emphasised. Problems appear less important when walking, swimming, running, cycling, or being involved in any other physical pursuit. This is because the mind is better able to maintain a proper perspective over events and situations when tension is released. Any activity that concentrates the attention on an interesting and enjoyable subject that is divorced from life's inherent problems will be beneficial in renewing inner strengths.

> Do not use sport to hone your competitive advantage. It is the taking part that counts, and not the winning.

HOW TO . . .

Exercise at Work

The following are useful exercises to perform at work – they are easy to follow and can easily be done at your desk.

They help to stretch the muscles, which can shorten due to overuse and repetitive strain, boost circulation, and help ease tension and stress by building up overused muscle groups.

Hand warm-up routine: This is an excellent routine for keyboard users or those who do a lot of writing.

- Shake your hands and wrists vigorously to increase mobility and circulation. Press the fingers back from the palms to the fullest limits, with your fingers held together.
- Gently press each finger back separately.
- Clench and relax your fists.
- Rotate your hands from the wrists with your fists clenched, and your elbows at the sides of your body.
- Always use a wrist protector band to alleviate pressure from keyboard edges. Some people like to use a long heated wheat bag to provide heat to sore and tired forearm muscles whilst typing.

Stretches to be Done During a Break Away From Your Desk

Neck and Head

- Gently let your head come down onto your chest and bring it back to the centre. Slowly rotate to the left so your chin rests on your left shoulder. Bring back to the centre and then rotate to the right and repeat the same procedure.

Shoulders

Clasp your hands behind your back and raise your arms towards your shoulders. You should feel a stretch at the front of your chest and shoulder area. This is a good exercise for opening up the chest and defusing tension.

- Raise your right arm so that it is against your right ear. Bend your arm so that your right hand is placed in the centre of your back between your shoulder blades. With your left hand, gently pull the arm further down so that your hand travels downwards. The stretch should be felt in your right arm and shoulders. Repeat on your left side.

- Clasp your hands in front of you and imagine that you are hugging a tree. Push outwards from the shoulders and you will feel a stretch across the back of your shoulders.

- Bring both arms out in front of you and then bring the left arm round to the left side and the right arm round to the right. Push behind with both arms and squeeze the shoulder blades together. The stretch should be felt on the front of your chest.

Lower Back

- Lie on the floor and bring your knees into your chest. Hold for a few seconds and then relax.

- Bring the right knee over to the left shoulder and repeat on the other side. This stretches the sides, back and stomach muscles, and is very good for lumber pain and sciatica.

Legs

The best exercise for the legs is to take regular breaks away from your desk. Walk around the office, take a trip to a colleague's office instead of phoning, and take the stairs instead of the lift. The calf muscle is vital in pumping and returning the blood back up from the feet to the trunk of the body, so any exercise which flexes the calf muscle is beneficial.

Foot rotation

Rotate and flex both feet. This will help flex the calf muscle and help with return of blood back to the heart via the veins.

Don't forget the eyes

- Rub your hands together to warm them, and then cup the eyes without pressing your hands to your eyes.

- Close your eyes and breathe deeply and slowly, visualising that you are looking into darkness.

This helps to relax the internal and external muscles of the eye. Also remember to take regular breaks away from your computer screen.

HOW TO . . .

Achieve Quality Relaxation

Regular periods of relaxation, in between or away from work schedules, are extremely important as they help to:

- Switch off the stress response
- Improve sleep patterns
- Reduce fatigue
- Increase self esteem

Relaxation gives you a chance to 'recharge your batteries'. In medical terms, during periods of relaxation, sympathetic nervous system activity is at its lowest - allowing the parasympathetic nervous system to increase its influence over body functions.

Accordingly, levels of noradrenaline, adrenaline and cortisol are low, and physical functions such as heart rate and breathing also decrease. When stressed, the muscles in your body tense and this muscular tension can cause headache, neck and shoulder discomfort, backache and so on.

These aches and pains can in turn increase tension, leading to a vicious circle of stress / tension and worry. Tension and relaxation are two sides of the same coin – you cannot experience both at the same time. You therefore need to learn to relax in order to switch off the effects of tension.

Relaxation techniques

Some people relax by doing something they have already discovered to be enjoyable, for example:

- Listening to music
- Reading
- Gardening
- Having a bath - perhaps with the addition of essential oils
- Watching a favourite film

There are also a range of more specific relaxation techniques that you can learn and use, some of the most popular of which include the following:

Paced breathing: The following are simple instructions for a technique that is especially beneficial for dealing with long-term stress and stressful situations and can also help with panic attacks, hyperventilation, breathlessness, dizziness, headaches and tension.

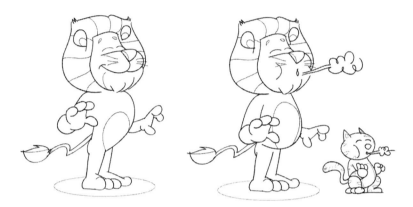

As the first step in learning the technique, you will need to set aside at least ten minutes twice a day to practice 'paced breathing'.

Basic Paced Breathing:

- Sit or lie down in a comfortable position away from the distractions of everyday life.

- Support your head with soft cushions so that the weight of your head is taken off your neck.

- Start to breathe regularly and slowly as if you were going to sleep, moving your stomach in and out (only your stomach should be moving, not your shoulders).

- It may be helpful to place a hand on your stomach to feel it moving as you breathe. Sometimes it can also be useful to practice in front of a mirror first.

- Place both hands on your diaphragm with your fingertips just touching. As you breathe you should be able to see your fingertips parting slightly as your diaphragm expands.

- In order to pace your breathing, it is advisable to practice this by breathing in to the count of 3 and then breathe out to the count of 3 (this should take 6 seconds).

- Continue this paced breathing for 2 minutes. Some people may find that initially this pattern of breathing may make them dizzy. If so, continue with the previous steps for a bit longer before introducing paced breathing.

- Gradually, you will be able to keep this paced breathing up for longer than 2 minutes. When you can keep this breathing rhythm for longer than 5 minutes you can begin to introduce some Progressive Muscle Relaxation techniques.

Progressive and deep muscular relaxation: This aims to reduce anxiety by emphasising physical relaxation. It consists of first tensing and then releasing all 16 major skeletal muscle groups in sequence.

At each stage, the mind concentrates initially on the feeling of tension and then on relaxation.

It should be noted that these techniques are not recommended for sufferers of hypertension (high blood pressure) since tensing of the muscles can elevate blood pressure.

Instructional CDs are available, and although the technique requires practice to become proficient, it enables the body to relax in stressful situations.

Meditation: This is based on the belief that we all have the capacity to interact with our inner self, and that meditation can be the key to gaining access to this centre of stillness. In the context of stress management, meditation therefore concentrates on relaxing the mind. There are a variety of methods, but the simplest one involves focusing for 20 minutes or more on a single word or sound, that is repeated over and over again in the mind, as a mantra.

> " *In the midst of movement and chaos, keep stillness inside of you.* "
>
> Deepak Chopra

Imagery: We may be able to imagine sitting on a beach, listening to the crashing waves and watching the sunset. We can sit there and forget all our problems, and in effect take ourselves off to another world - a perfect way of relieving stress from our bodies. This is, in effect, a type of auto-suggestion that allows us to indulge our senses and let the pleasure bring relief from our problems. This is a scene that we can bring to the forefront of our minds at any time - even sitting behind a desk.

'You' time: It is important for all of us to ensure that we make at least a modicum of time for ourselves each day. With 16 waking hours in a day, it should be possible to reserve 20 minutes solely for ourselves. When you look in your diary, it is unlikely you will find your own name appearing in it because it will be full of everyone else's – so allocate time to yourself and make sure you keep your appointment.

> **"** *Don't underestimate the value of doing nothing, of just going along, listening to all the things you can't hear, and not bothering.* **"**
>
> Pooh's Little Instruction Book, inspired by A.A. Milne

Having a warm bath: Water seems to have special powers when it comes to minimising stress and rejuvenating our bodies. It has a beneficial effect on relaxing the skin and muscles, and calms the lungs, heart, stomach and endocrine system by stimulating nerve reflexes. Heat generally soothes the body, slowing down the activity of internal organs. Cold stimulates and invigorates, increasing internal activity.

> **"** *There must be quite a few things that a hot bath won't cure, but I don't know many of them.* **"**
>
> Sylvia Plath, The Bell Jar

If you are experiencing tense muscles and anxiety from stress, a hot shower or bath will often help. Follow this with an invigorating cold shower and this will help stimulate your mind and body.

Experiment with different water temperatures and times, to determine what suits you and your body best.

" *Peace comes from within. Do not seek it without.* **"**
Buddha

HOW TO . . .

Take 'Time Out'

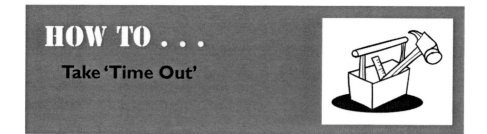

Being physically active - walking, stretching or even enjoying your environment can be effective 'stress-busters'. This is why it is so important to take regular breaks away from situations or tasks that are sources of stress and frustration.

Although this will not solve the root cause of your stress, it gives you an opportunity to think about the situation more objectively and may even help you to resolve it by looking at it from a different perspective.

Relax Quickly - Everyday

Even if you do not have time for all of the techniques mentioned earlier, there are a number of techniques you can use to help your body to stay relaxed.

1. When you feel the urge to **stretch**, doing so will help to release tension. Trust your urge to stretch and give yourself some quick relaxation.

2. Try not to suppress the desire to **yawn**. A good yawn will stretch and relax your face, neck and shoulder muscles. It is also nature's way of telling you your body is tired, and will help to give you more oxygen with which to re-energise your body.

3. When your legs and feet feel tired after a long day, you naturally want to rub your feet. Follow this urge and **massage your feet**. Rotate your feet and ankles slowly, as this will help to relax your feet naturally.

   Or, place your feet under warm running water, or in a bowl of warm water with smooth pebbles to massage the reflex points on your soles.

4. If you feel anger rising in your chest or tears beginning, **breathe** in to the count of four and then breathe out to the count of four or even more. Be sure to breathe from the diaphragm (as previously mentioned). Many people take a bit longer to breathe out than to breathe in, and this is even more relaxing. Repeat this six times or more and you will be more in control of your emotions, more relaxed and better able to deal with the situation.

5. Anywhere, and at any time of the day, stop and take one **deep breath**. This will help to revitalise your body and strengthen a good habit of breathing properly.

6. An excellent de-tenser and refresher is a 15-30 minute **brisk walk** in the open air. As your breathing deepens so more oxygen can be supplied, increasing your body's ability to work properly for you.

7. Any **change** of activity is helpful when you are feeling stressed or emotional. Get up and get a glass of water, cup of tea, coffee or a soft drink (remembering to keep your caffeine levels down), or go and talk to someone.

HOW TO . . .

Sleep Soundly

It is well known that sleep has a major role to play in helping the body to repair itself both physically and mentally, so not surprisingly it is also widely acknowledged that sleep deprivation can be a major cause of stress.

The following **8 key strategies** will help you obtain benefit from the 'good sleep' that you need to function at maximum levels:

1. Try not to just lie in bed fretting when you cannot sleep. Get out of bed and perhaps make a warm drink, or do something you enjoy and that relaxes you. Consider relaxation techniques such as progressive muscular relaxation, visualisation etc.

2. Keep a pencil and paper next to your bed and write down an outline of anything that wakes you. It may be something you need to remember to do the next day, or you never know, it could be an amazingly innovative idea that you may forget by the morning if you don't capture it at that very moment.

3. If you have a tendency to wake up with your 'to do' list in your mind, try getting up and writing about what may be bothering you. If your 'to do' list continues to go round and round in your head, try writing lists **before** you leave work or start getting ready to go to bed.

4. If the same thoughts return in the night, tell them to go away and distract yourself with other thoughts, e.g. build up a clear visual picture of the design of your ideal garden or house, or mentally visualise a pleasant holiday or social occasion.

5. If you wake in the night, don't keep looking at the clock. Watching the time go by will only increase your anxiety and postpone sleep for even longer.

6. Ensure caffeine consumption is kept to a minimum, and avoid drinking tea and coffee in the evenings. More than five cups of coffee a day, or ten cups of tea, can increase the pulse rate and disturb sleep patterns.

7. Prior to going to bed, try to take your mind off the problems of the day. Read a book, listen to some soothing music, watch an amusing film or do some other relaxing activity.

8. Eating heavy meals late at night or going to bed hungry are not to be encouraged. There should be at least a two-hour space between finishing a meal and going to sleep.

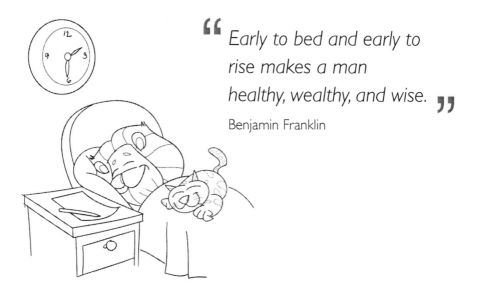

 " *Early to bed and early to rise makes a man healthy, wealthy, and wise.* "

Benjamin Franklin

HOW TO . . .
Improve Your Leisure Time

A very important way to relax is to take time out to enjoy hobbies or increase leisure time. It does not matter what you do - it is the making time away from work or family stresses that is important.

Some hobbies can give a wonderful sense of achievement that is not available in other areas of life – for example learning to play an instrument or even climbing or flying an aeroplane. These activities allow the mind to focus on achieving an enjoyable goal and ceasing to dwell on everyday stress.

It is common nowadays to hear someone say, 'I really enjoy singing, dancing, walking, sailing, but I don't seem to have the time to do it anymore.' To have a well balanced work and home life, it is important to make time for activities that you enjoy. Some people feel incredibly guilty about making time for their hobby or themselves. This is particularly true with working parents, who feel that every spare moment should be spent with their children.

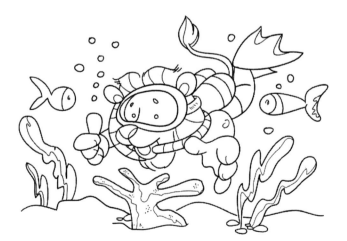

So why not get the whole family involved in a hobby or leisure activity? By focusing on something completely different, it is entirely possible to feel more energised. Many people have even turned their hobbies into successful careers - proving the saying that if you enjoy something you are probably very good at it.

No. 3. Changing Your Mindset

Changing your mindset is such a wide-ranging topic that it more than merits being the subject of a book in its own right. And indeed, many books have been written on the subject – several of which are recommended under 'Individual Stress Awareness' in the 'Read More About It' section on page 243.

In broad terms, however, the way in which you **perceive** situations is as important as how you respond to them. How you think is therefore an area in which you can make proactive interventions, including:

- Modifying your perspective

- Developing a positive attitude

- Banishing negative self-talk

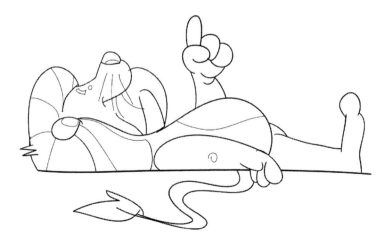

HOW TO . . .

Modify Your Perspective

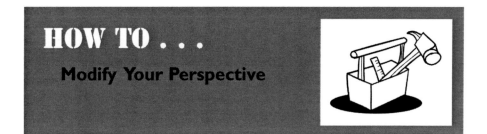

It is very helpful to be able to reflect and modify your thinking so that you can improve the way you perceive events and relate to others.

There are many ways of interpreting a situation – one of the best known being 'is the glass half empty or half full?'. Some people will always see the negative aspect and others the positive. It can therefore be useful to ask, 'is there another way of seeing this situation?'.

For example, if you come into contact with a person in a position of authority, do you always react in a particular way? Do you pre-plan how you will react to certain situations, and then find that the reality bears no relation to what you expected? Do you think of change at work as a threat to your status, or an opportunity for self development? Are there people who you always feel negative towards, irrespective of how they behave towards you?

If your answers to any of these questions is 'yes', it may be worth considering whether modifying your perspective would assist you in these situations. And as always, it is important to learn from each event - what was helpful and unhelpful about the situation and how you viewed it.

" *The mind is everything. What you think - you become.* **"**
Buddha

HOW TO . . .
Develop a Positive Attitude

The power of positive thinking can help you resist feelings of hopelessness, desperation and failure. That is why it is important to focus on your strengths and to look for, and seize, opportunities that could result from a particular situation or set of circumstances.

It is natural to think about what the future may hold, but it is important to retain a proper perspective. It is pointless to worry excessively about future events – 'what might happen if'...

The future has not taken place yet and there will inevitably be large parts of it over which you have no control.

In addition, worrying about a possible negative outcome will simply increase anxiety and tension, whereas focusing on a positive outcome will reduce this tension and so help you to achieve your goals.

A practical way of doing this is as follows:

- Write down the worst scenario possible
- Consider (truthfully) the likelihood of it occurring
- Imagine the best scenario possible
- Put together a plan that maximises the likelihood of the best scenario and minimises the likelihood of the worst
- Try to remember similar situations in the past which at first seemed just as threatening, but ultimately turned out well.

The learning curve is to try to recognise and accept when a situation is beyond your control, focus on what you can do positively and keep on practicing.

8 Useful Tips to Improve Your Life

1. Value the relationships you have in your life. Nourish them and put effort into them.

2. Don't let your problems overwhelm you. Keep them in perspective and think for a moment of those that are so much worse off than you.

3. Recognise when you are thinking negatively about yourself, and change your perspective by considering what is real and what is your perception.

4. Try not to exaggerate your problems and underestimate your ability to solve them.

5. The best things in life are often free. Enjoy the simple pleasures of life.

6. Laughter is a wonderful medicine and it can lift your spirits when they are at their lowest ebb. Smile a little and you will see others smiling too.

7. Put a positive spin on your problems and look for new opportunities. A change of direction may be just what you need.

8. Look adversity in the eye. Face up to your fears and insecurities about the unknown and grab opportunities as they present themselves. Life may never be the same again - but it may be even better.

9. Focus on what you want to achieve in the future – rather than what you think may be threatening or stopping you. You can't change the past but you can certainly learn from it.

10. Develop some personal mantras – 'I can' and 'I will'.

HOW TO . . .

Banish Negative Self-Talk

Much of the distress that individuals experience is caused by negative thoughts, their expectations of themselves and other people, and what they think others are expecting of them.

It is often very constructive for people to think about what they tell themselves – and the internal language they use.

Even simple phrases such as, 'I shouldn't be saying this, but …' or 'I know I haven't got the right to say this, but …' reveal a lot about how people perceive themselves in relation to those around them, their self esteem and aspects of their lives that may therefore be causing them stress.

> Many individuals cause themselves undue stress by inappropriate 'self-talk'.

Unfortunately, negative self-talk tends to be a self-fulfilling prophecy. It isn't easy to challenge our internal language, especially when we're feeling bad about ourselves, but it is possible to do this by:

- Checking whether what we think is real. If we were sitting in a court, what hard evidence would we have to support the way we're thinking? What evidence is there to support the opposite view?

- Changing our perspective. How would we perceive the situation if we were feeling positive about ourselves rather than negative?

- Putting things into proportion. Are they as bad as we're making them out to be? Will they matter next week, next month or in a year's time?

- Looking for positives. Is the way we're thinking actually helping us? What can we do that will solve the problem or improve the situation?

" *The last of human freedoms - the ability to chose one's attitude in a given set of circumstances.* **"**

Viktor Frankl

Additional Stress-busting Resources

Executive Summary of Proven Tools and Techniques

Stress has many causes, and affects people in a variety of ways. In the workplace, stress can have devastating effects, not just on the individual but on the organisation as a whole. Where an employee is suffering any combination of the emotional, physical and behavioural symptoms which stress induces, performance will clearly suffer, and this in turn may well affect others within the organisation.

Although stressful situations are sometimes unavoidable, it is very often possible both for management to foresee and pre-empt their occurrence, and for employees to learn to effectively cope with the consequent pressure. A proactive management culture can avoid the worst effects of stress by means of risk assessment, improved communication, ongoing performance reviews, education and training.

- Stress is the reaction to an inappropriate amount of pressure or responsibility when the individual being subjected to these feels inadequate and unable to cope.

- Pressure provides the stimulation and challenge that we all use to achieve job satisfaction and self esteem. An optimum amount of pressure assists performance but if it develops into stress, then performance will be affected.

- Excessive pressure is not 'good for you'.

- To suffer from stress is not 'a sign of weakness'.

- The ability to control circumstance, i.e. to have some input over events, is generally accepted to be an important contributor to a sense of wellbeing in the individual. This understanding has led to the development of management interventions which assist individuals to cope with pressure when it turns into stress.

- Stress manifests itself in cognitive, psychological, physiological and behavioural changes.

- Everyone responds to stress to a different degree and in their own way.

- It is possible to learn to manage stress successfully, rather than allowing it to overwhelm you to an extent where your physical and mental health is damaged.

- Avoiding the effects of excessive stress requires you to identify those stressors which affect you personally and learn how to control them, either by yourself or with professional help.

- What is accepted as a motivating pressure for you may manifest itself as stress to others, and what may appear to you as stressful one day may actually be seen as a positive pressure the next.

- Stress is like a light switch, your mind turns it on automatically but you need to learn how to turn it off.

In order to get the most from life, it is important for all of us to try to maintain a balance between stimulation and relaxation, exercise and rest, responsibility and freedom, work and play, laughter and tears. This is not easy, but there is a wide range of proactive interventions that we can implement in order to improve the balance in our lives.

- A 'stress diary' can be invaluable in helping you to understand not only the major sources of stress - but also the frequency with which they are being experienced.

- It is important to try to alter the balance in your activities from being 'stress producing' to 'stress reducing'.

- If you find it difficult to say 'no', assertiveness and time management training can both be extremely valuable.

- How you manage your time is a key factor in determining how stressful your life can be.

- Humour gives you a different perspective on your problems. If you can make light of a situation, then it can become less threatening.

- It is important to take regular breaks away from situations or tasks that are the source of stress and frustration.

- The proactive interventions you can make to help develop a healthier lifestyle include changes related to diet, exercise, relaxation, sleep and leisure.

- A well balanced diet is crucial in preserving health and helping to reduce stress, but there are certain foods and drinks that act as powerful stimulants to the body and can contribute to stress.

- It is important to limit your caffeine intake, as this 'kick starts' the stress reaction.

- You should aim to keep the consumption of 'convenience' foods to the minimum, as many contain large amounts of sugar, salt, fat and preservatives.

- It is essential that you drink at least two litres of water per day.

- Exercise can be good for both your body and your mind, and it is thought that stress poses significantly less danger to the overall health of people who are physically fit.

- It is extremely important that you include a daily period of relaxation in your life.

> Tension and relaxation are two sides of the same coin – you cannot experience both at the same time. You therefore need to learn to turn on the bodily effects of relaxation so that you can turn off the symptoms of tension.

- Proactive interventions regarding how you think about things including changing your perspective, positive thinking and self-talk can provide a basis for change.

- Exercise provides an outlet for negative emotions (such as frustration and anger) to be dispersed. It is important to choose an activity that you enjoy so that you increase your chances of maintaining it.

- In recent years, a wide range of 'alternative' therapies have been offered for the treatment of stress. Depending on method, mode and the individual, some will be more effective than others.

And don't forget...

- To make time for your friends and family – talking, sharing, enjoying your moments and making them special...

Carole's 12 Point Anti-Stress Checklist for Busy Executives

1. Walk away from situations that you have no control over. Write down what was causing you stress and physically draw a line under it.

2. Park your email. Turn off your email alerts as they interrupt what you are doing. Set time aside daily to do your correspondence. Interruptions break your concentration and make you less effective.

3. Compartmentalise activity. Draw up a quadrant and put your activities into a box. From there you will see what overspills into each activity.

4. When things go wrong, take the positive learning that comes out of the situation and move on. Don't dwell on the past - what could have been. Don't go into victim mode.

5. Draw up your 'to do' list at the end of each day ready for the next. Make sure you start each week with a revised list.

6. Prioritise your tasks and put deadline dates next to each one.

7. Put some 'me time' into your diary each day. Think about how many times <u>your</u> name appears in <u>your</u> diary!

8. Choose an exercise activity that you enjoy or you won't stick to it.

9. Share your goals with a colleague or friend so that you are accountable to someone else. That way you will ensure it happens.

10. Know how many hours sleep you need per night and ensure you get it. If you have to get up early in the morning then get an early night.

11. Use your 'dead' time effectively. You can always use this time as thinking time.

12. Communicate and ask for help when you need it. People aren't mind readers – you have to ask for support!

Once upon a time...

A professor began his class by holding up a glass with some water in it.

He held it up for all to see and asked the students, 'How much do you think this glass weighs?'

'50 grams!'... '100 grams!'... '125 grams' ... the students answered.

'I really don't know unless I weigh it,' said the professor, 'but my question is: what would happen if I held it up like this for a few minutes?'

'Nothing,' the students said.

'OK! What would happen if I held it up like this for an hour?' the professor asked.

'Your arm would begin to ache,' said one of the students.

'You are right. Now what would happen if I held it for a day?'

'Your arm could go numb, you might have severe muscle stress and paralysis and have to go to hospital for sure!' ventured another student; and all the students laughed.

'Very good. But during all this, did the weight of the glass change?' asked the professor.

'No,' was the answer.

'Then what caused the arm ache and the muscle stress?'

The students were puzzled.

'Holding on to the glass and not putting it down,' said one of the students.

'Exactly!' said the professor. 'Life's problems are something like this. Hold them for a few minutes in your head and they seem OK.

'Think of them for a long time and they begin to ache. Hold them even longer and they begin to paralyse you. You will not be able to do anything.

'It's important to think of the challenges in your life, but EVEN MORE IMPORTANT is to "PUT THEM DOWN" at the end of every day before you go to sleep.

'That way, you are not stressed, you wake up every day fresh and strong and can handle any issue, any challenge that comes your way!'

So, when you leave the office today, remember to 'PUT THE GLASS DOWN TODAY'...

Exercise # 11

Your New Anti-Stress Philosophy

Spend some time thinking about situations which you find personally stressful. These can be either at work or at home.

When you have identified these, consider ways in which you could make these situations less stressful.

For instance, would being better prepared or more assertive reduce the level of stress you experience?

Would practising some relaxation techniques such as deep breathing help you cope more effectively?

Being clear now will really help when you are faced with this situation again.

Now complete the following grid, as honestly and as creatively as you can.

How will you cope now With Stressful Situations

Spend some time thinking about situations which you find personally stressful. These can be either at work or at home.

When you have identified these, consider ways in which you could make these situations less stressful.

For instance, would being better prepared or more assertive reduce the level of stress you experience?

Would practising some relaxation techniques such as deep breathing help you cope more effectively?

Being clear now will really help when you are faced with this situation again.

Now complete the following grid, as honestly and as creatively as you can.

Stressful Situation	Coping Strategy

Personal Stress Management Contract

Complete this contract and maintain your goals.

I could avoid or ease the impact of stress in my life if I were to start:

I could avoid or ease the impact of stress in my life if I were to stop:

I will know that I am managing my stress better when I find myself:

Exercise # 13

Business Stress Management Contract

Complete this contract and maintain your goals.

I could avoid or ease the impact of stress in my team if I were to start:

_____
_____
_____
_____
_____

I could avoid or ease the impact of stress in my team if I were to stop:

_____
_____
_____
_____
_____

I will know that I am managing stress better when I find my team:

_____
_____
_____
_____

Don't Feel Frustrated at not Being a World-Class Leader

Not everyone can be President – but you can strive to be in the presidential team!

Work in an age of community - to be an integral part of society is to be accepted by your peers and that is fundamental to your success.

'Employee Engagement' is what great Managers do - they cannot be truly successful without it.

Wear your 'Vision of Excellence' badge with pride - without vision you are blind, and without excellence you are merely average.

Weave your employees into the fabric of your company - a cloth that is frayed eventually tears.

Be the person that others emulate - everyone needs a role model who is an exemplar.

Love what you do, love the challenge - love is the strongest force that we humans possess.

Engage, involve and inspire your team, carry them with you - a bundle of matches cannot be broken but a single match snaps easily.

10 Quick Stress Management Fixes

If you have the kind of 'Type A' personality traits that lead you to read the end of a book before the beginning, here are ten quick stress management 'fixes' that will immediately make a difference to your life and your ability to cope with stress…

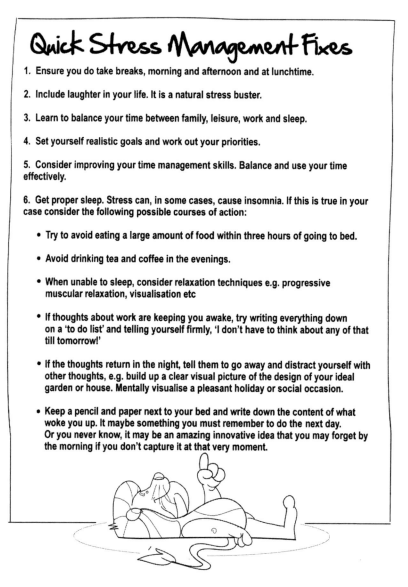

Quick Stress Management Fixes

1. Ensure you do take breaks, morning and afternoon and at lunchtime.

2. Include laughter in your life. It is a natural stress buster.

3. Learn to balance your time between family, leisure, work and sleep.

4. Set yourself realistic goals and work out your priorities.

5. Consider improving your time management skills. Balance and use your time effectively.

6. Get proper sleep. Stress can, in some cases, cause insomnia. If this is true in your case consider the following possible courses of action:

- Try to avoid eating a large amount of food within three hours of going to bed.

- Avoid drinking tea and coffee in the evenings.

- When unable to sleep, consider relaxation techniques e.g. progressive muscular relaxation, visualisation etc

- If thoughts about work are keeping you awake, try writing everything down on a 'to do list' and telling yourself firmly, 'I don't have to think about any of that till tomorrow!'

- If the thoughts return in the night, tell them to go away and distract yourself with other thoughts, e.g. build up a clear visual picture of the design of your ideal garden or house. Mentally visualise a pleasant holiday or social occasion.

- Keep a pencil and paper next to your bed and write down the content of what woke you up. It maybe something you must remember to do the next day. Or you never know, it may be an amazing innovative idea that you may forget by the morning if you don't capture it at that very moment.

... and for the eagle-eyed among you, the 10th 'quick fix' is that to ensure you turn your good intentions into positive changes, every action you choose to take should have a deadline by which you commit to achieving it!

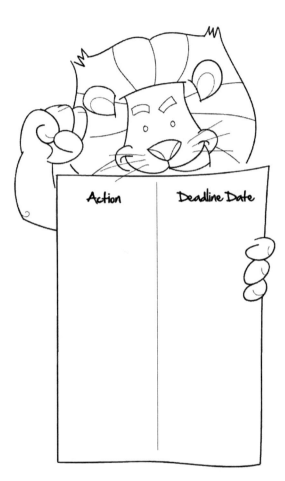

Once upon a time...

The first day of school, our professor introduced himself and challenged us to get to know someone whom we didn't already know. I stood up to look around when a gentle hand touched my shoulder. I turned around to find a wrinkled little old lady beaming up at me with a smile that lit up her entire being. She said, 'Hi Handsome! My name is Rose. I'm eighty-seven years old. Can I give you a hug?' I laughed and enthusiastically responded, 'Of course you may!' and she gave me a giant squeeze.

'Why are you in college at such a young, innocent age?' I asked. She jokingly replied, 'I'm here to meet a rich husband, get married, have a couple of kids...'

'No seriously,' I asked. I was curious what may have motivated her to be taking on this challenge at her age.

'I always dreamed of having a college education and now I'm finally getting one!' she told me.

After class we walked to the student union building, shared a chocolate milkshake and became instant friends. Every day, for the next three months, we would leave class together and talk non-stop, about the world and about our families and friends.

I was always mesmerized listening to this 'time machine' as she shared her wisdom and experience with me.

Over the course of the year, Rose became a campus icon and she easily made friends wherever she went. She loved to dress up and she revelled in the attention bestowed upon her from the other students. She was enjoying her college time to the full.

At the end of the semester we invited Rose to speak at our football banquet. I'll never forget what she taught us. She was introduced and stepped up to the podium.

As she began to deliver her prepared speech, she dropped her speech notes on the floor. Frustrated and a little embarrassed, she leaned into the microphone and simply said, 'I'm sorry I'm so jittery. I gave up beer for Lent and this whiskey is killing me! I'll never get my speech back in order, so let me just tell you what I know.'

As we laughed she cleared her throat and began, 'We do not stop playing because we are old; we grow old because we stop playing. There are simple secrets to staying young, being happy and achieving success:

'You have to laugh and find humour every day. You've got to have a dream. When you lose your dreams, you die. We have so many people walking around who are dead and don't even know it!

'There is a huge difference between growing older and growing up. If you are nineteen years old and lie in bed for one full year and don't do one productive thing, you will turn twenty years old.

'If I am eighty-seven years old and stay in bed for a year and never do anything, I will turn eighty-eight. Anybody can grow older.

'That doesn't take any talent or ability. The idea is to grow up by always finding the opportunity in change and to have no regrets. The only people who fear death are those with regrets.'

She concluded her speech by courageously singing 'The Rose.' She challenged each of us to study the lyrics and live them out in our daily lives.

At the year's end, Rose finished the college degree she had begun all those years ago.

One week after graduation, Rose died peacefully in her sleep.

Over two thousand college students attended her funeral in tribute to the wonderful woman who taught, by example, that it's never too late to be all you can possibly be.

These words have been written in loving memory of ROSE.

I wish I could have met her. But we can all be like her – if we keep on learning and dreaming and living life to the full.

A Postscript

I was sent this story of Rose by a colleague who knew that I would appreciate it. It proves to me that anything in life is possible if we want it to be. I never met Rose, but if any reader of this book did, then please contact me with your story of her and the legacy that she left.

It is a fact that stress can get in the way of our achieving success and that is one of the reasons why I decided to write this book. Today, life has become frenetic and the speed at which we live and work has become supercharged with many of us expecting to be on call 24/7.

Swim with the current and not against it ...

Can we change this? In some ways we can but in other ways we have to learn how to swim with the current and not against it – all the time being aware that there are both **'fish and rocks'** in the water. The first can feed us and keep us healthy, the second can damage and hurt us. We need to keep a continuous watch out for both. If we ignore either, then we will never get to where we want to swim towards and, in extreme circumstances, we could even drown.

For myself, I know that my living and my working are entwined (you ask my children!). I cannot imagine any day without writing, reading or increasing my experience and enriching my life. I know that I need the stimulation of curiosity and work and the growth that it brings through the knowledge learned; the satisfaction of a job well done and the opportunity of giving to others.

Love what you do...

The key for me are the words of poet Khalil Gibran, 'Work is love made visible'. If you love what you do, then it often doesn't matter how hard you work and that the boundaries of work and home sometimes merge. However, you do need a sensible work-life balance and to know how and when to switch off. All this is part of how we manage the pressures of our daily life to ensure that they do not turn into destructive stress.

So wherever you are in the world, whichever country, whichever culture – you need to watch out for both the **'fish'** and the **'rocks'**.

Whether I am working in the fast-paced environment of Dubai, the rich culture of the townships of the Southern Cape of South Africa, or the frenetic City of London, I am constantly aware that I need to balance what I do, how I do it, and to value my time.

'Walk the walk' as well as 'talk the talk' ...

Research has shown that only a limited percentage of people ever get to read the end of a book, so if you have arrived at this page, then I thank you for giving me the opportunity of taking you onto the next stage of your journey with me on how to effectively manage your stress.

It really is your choice now to 'walk the walk', rather than simply 'talk the talk'. You possess a much broader array of tools and skills than you did when you opened the first page of this book, but it's up to you how and when you use them.

From now on, it's all about doing what you say you're going to do, and turning your ideas into actions. Ultimately, nobody has more control over your life than you do.

And Don't Forget....

Switching off - Don't let those long-running problems invade your whole day and night. Learn to lock them away and move onto other good things in your life.

Traffic frustration - Instead of feeling victimised, think of those people all over the world who will never enjoy the blessings of owning a car.

Bad day at work - Think of the thousands of unemployed who cannot find any work and who would view your position with envy, whatever its irritations.

Stormy love life - If your relationship has hit a bad patch, consider the bleak emotional state of the person who has never found love.

Taking work home - A weekend spoiled? In another part of the world, you might be the person working twelve hours a day, every day, just to live and eat.

Having to walk it - Missed the last bus? Think of the paraplegic who would love be in a fit state to take that walk, however long.

Age worries - If a few grey hairs make you feel depressed, think of the cancer patient in chemotherapy who only wishes they had some hair to comb.

What's it all about - If you fall to pondering the meaning of life, be thankful you've actually got a life to examine at your leisure.

Suffering other people's bitterness - It could be worse. You could have sunk to their level of insecurity and small-mindedness.

Carpe Diem. Quam minimum credula postero. (Seize the day; put no trust in tomorrow.) Horace

…and remember to live life to the full and enjoy every moment of every day and show stress who's boss!

Carole

Carole Spiers

Read More About It!

Organisational Stress

Tolley's Managing Stress in the Workplace
By Carole Spiers (published by LexisNexis). An essential manager's handbook to help manage work-related stress. ISBN 0-7545-1269-X (2003) www.carolespiersgroup.co.uk or www.amazon.co.uk

Real Solutions, Real People: Tackling Work-Related Stress
An HSE publication, including case study prompt cards to be used in discussion groups.
HSE Books (2003) Tel: 01787 881165 ISBN 0 71762767 5
www.hsebooks.co.uk

Intervention in Occupational Stress
By Randall R Ross and Elizabeth M Altmaier
Sage Publications (1994) ISBN 0-8039-8673-4

Managing Workplace Stress
By Cary L Cooper and Susan Cartwright
Sage Publications (1997) ISBN 0-7619-0193-0

Managing Employee Stress in the Workplace
By Lesley Towner
Kogan Page (1997) ISBN 0-7494-2526-1

The Stress Workbook: How Individuals Teams and Organisations can Balance Pressure and Performance
By Eve Warren & Caroline Toll
Nicholas Brealey (1996) ISBN 1-85788-171-0

Stress - A Management Guide
By John Clark
Published by Spiro Business Guides (2002)
ISBN 1-904298-29-X

Meeting the Stress Challenge: A Training and Staff Development Manual
By Neil Thompson, Michael Murphy and Steve Stradling
Russell House Publishing (1998) ISBN 1-898924-47-3

Emotional and Physiological Processes and Positive Intervention Strategies (Research in Occupational Stress and Well Being)
By Daniel C. Ganster, Pamela L. Perrewe
JAI Press (2003) ISBN 0-76231057-X

Counselling for Occupational Stress: A Handbook of Counselling for Stress at Work
By Randall R Ross and Elizabeth M Altmaier
Sage Publications (1994) ISBN 0-8039-8673-4

Coping With Stress at Work
By Jacqueline M. Atkinson
HarperCollins (1994) ISBN 0-7225-3095-1

**Managing Workplace Stress: A Best Practice Blueprint
(CBI Fast Track S.)**
By Stephen Williams and Lesley Cooper
John Wiley and Sons Ltd (2002) ISBN 0-47084-287-3

Individual Stress Awareness

Being Happy
By Andrew Matthews
A light hearted look at stress, helping you to understand yourself, forgive yourself and understand life in general.
ISBN 978-9810006648

Follow Your Heart – Finding Purpose in Your Life and Work
By Andrew Matthews
A book to help you through your life and to learn how to do the things you love and deal with the occasional disaster. ISBN 0-646 31066-6

Think Your Way to Happiness
By Dr Windy Dryden & Jack Gordon
Learn to understand your feelings and see that you don't have to feel bad about things. ISBN 0-85969-603-0

Build Your Own Rainbow
By Barrie Hopson and Mike Scally
Does what it says in the title, helps the reader through a series of exercises to plan their personal and career objectives.
ISBN 978-1852523008

The Don't Sweat the Small Stuff Work Book
By Richard Carlson
The practical workbook companion to Carlson's best selling book 'Don't Sweat the Small Stuff' full of practical tips and advice. ISBN 0-340-73833-2

I'm Not Crazy, I'm Just Not You

By Roger Pearlman & Sara C Albritton

An explanation of the 16 Myers Briggs personality types which help us to understand and work alongside our colleagues.

ISBN 978-1857885521

What You Think of Me is None of My Business

By Terry Cole-Whittaker

A helpful book that increases the reader's self awareness and builds self esteem.

ISBN 978-0515094794

Happiness Now!

By Robert Holden

Hodder Mobius (1999) ISBN 0-3407-1309-7

'Turn Your Passion Into Profit!'

Inspirational Book of Self-Marketing

If You're Wanting Sustainable Success ... Wanting Is Not Enough!

What is being said about 'Turn Your Passion into Profit'

'To use an overworked phrase, but in this case true, I found your talk 'truly inspiring'. It helped me to bring back into focus what I was in business for. So much so that in 2 days I had overhauled my marketing strategy and begun to put it into practice. I now keep your book 'Turn Passion into Profit' on my desk as an invaluable reference tool.' *Sheila Germain, Sheila Rose Accessories*

'I bought Carole's book 'Turn Your Passion Into Profit' and it gave me skills, tools and strategies and would highly recommend it to anyone looking to market themselves or their business.' *Claire Naylor, Forward Financial Solutions*

'Positive Action Against Stress'
Instant Stress Relief Tips

Handy pocket manual giving clear overview of this topical subject

What is being said about 'Positive Action Against Stress'

'Proven tips by a proven expert. A brilliant book to dip into and keep in my desk drawer. It has helped me time and time again providing knowledge and tips to help me manage my stress better.' *Colin Dale, CEO, Business Information.*

e-Books

Discover the 20-secrets to a Stress-Free Year!
Imagine a year without Stress!

'The Silent Scream'
Coping with short and long-term effects of trauma

'Taking the Stress out of Driving'
Are you a SAFE Driver?

Train the Trainer Toolkits and PowerPoint Slides

All training packs include delegate workbook for copying in any number and PowerPoint slides for immediate use.

Managing Workplace Bullying and Harassment: *'Back-off!'*
Intervening to deter unacceptable behaviours

Time Management: *'Hurry...Hurry...Every Second Counts'*
Not just saving seconds, re-shaping your working life!

Crisis Intervention: *'Trauma Strikes When it Likes!....'*
Understand the foundations of trauma management

Interpersonal Communications: *'What to Say When you Don't Know What to Say'*
The essential conversation system.

Anger Management and Conflict Resolution: *'Cool it'*.
Highly-prized techniques
for defusing aggression.

To order any of these titles or to find out information about the complete range of services available from Carole Spiers, please visit our website.

If you would like to receive Carole's weekly column in Gulf News delivered directly to your desk, please visit our website and register today.

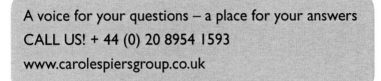

A voice for your questions – a place for your answers
CALL US! + 44 (0) 20 8954 1593
www.carolespiersgroup.co.uk

About the Author

Carole Spiers MIHPE, MISMA
Leading Authority on Corporate Stress.
Motivational Speaker.
BBC Guest-Broadcaster.
Best-selling Author.

As a leading authority on Executive Stress, popular BBC Guest-Broadcaster, Carole's focus is on developing a healthy workplace culture through the successful management of stress and organisational change – all of which is underpinned by a compelling philosophy reinforced by her own experience as an Expert Witness before the UK Courts.

Author of industry's bible 'Tolley's Managing Stress in the Workplace', Carole's credibility is rooted in twenty years success as CEO of the Carole Spiers Group, an International Stress Management and Employee Wellbeing consultancy, working with equal success with leading corporations in the contrasting cultures of the UK and the Gulf.

Carole has also established herself as a provocative, weekly columnist for the prestigious Gulf News, the Emirates leading daily newspaper, writing on topical issues facing Middle East Management.

She is Past President of the London Chapter of the Professional Speaking Association, and in 1999 Carole launched the UK's highly successful media campaign, National Stress Awareness Day on behalf of the International Stress Management Association UK, of which she was a Past Chair.

Carole is a high-energy motivational speaker able to combine inspiration with insight. Her charismatic style and ability to engage emotionally with audiences has made her a sought-after keynote speaker around the world. Her inspirational style and range of high-impact presentations are equally suitable as a curtain-raiser, closing speech or major keynote. With her vibrant personality and unique flair for establishing rapport with any audience, she handles sensitive issues with empathy and understanding born out of experience, encouraging that crucial two-way dialogue that brings about a positive change in people's lives.

She is also regularly called upon by the national and international press and media for comment.

Pro-bono Work

Carole has repeatedly visited battle-zones to train humanitarian aid workers in crisis intervention and post trauma stress, as well as to counsel refugees. Carole was also a Samaritan for over 20 years on its vital telephone listening service. For the past 8 years, Carole has motivated and inspired local entrepreneurs in South African townships and provided marketing expertise for those wishing to develop their businesses in Western Cape Communities.

On a personal note: Carole's three children are the love of her life and seeing the growth of her grandchildren gives her immeasurable pride and joy.

During the long summer days, she spends many hours in her London garden, growing flowers and picking fruit – and in the winter evenings, her passion is the Royal Opera House in London's West End, to listen to Puccini and Verdi.

What is Being Said About Carole Spiers From Around the World

'Your energy and experience was greatly appreciated...the value you added was immeasurable. Your presentation was intelligent, interactive and energetic - just what we needed as the closing keynote to our Family Business Forum in Abu Dhabi.'
Purva Hassomal, Director. Leaders of Abu Dhabi, Family Business Forum

'Carole's presentation has been extremely useful to both staff and managers alike. Feedback from delegates has without exception been very positive. It has helped to build relationships and open communications throughout the team, and I know I have a more equipped team as a result.'
Richard Farrer. AXA Insurance

'Thank you for providing us with an excellent insight into stress management.'
Brendan Noonan, Senior Vice President Training and Development, Emirates Airline Group.

'I expect that Carole's book 'Tolley's Managing Stress in the Workplace' will be compulsory reading for all HR Managers and Directors, as well as company secretaries and business managers with responsibilities for people.'
Keith Lawson. Consultant with the Centre for Management and Personal Development

'You were an outstanding Chair of the International Stress Management Association from 2001 – 2002 and I am glad to hear that you will stay as one of our Vice Presidents.'
Prof Cary L Cooper CBE. Professor of Organisational Psychology and Health. Lancaster University Management School.

'I just wanted to thank you for doing such a superb job as President of the London chapter of the Professional Speakers Association from 2006 - 2008. You have raised the bar and we are all in your debt.'
Barry Graham. Past President of the London Chapter of the Professional Speakers Association

'Carole delivered the final keynote on entrepreneurship to our European convention and here is a lady who lives and breathes enterprise in every aspect of her delivery.'
Peter Rossegg, Marketing Manager, Re/Max Europe

Stress Management Training, Workplace Counselling and Consultancy at the Service of Commerce and Industry

"Our mission is to empower organisations to achieve sustainable success through a healthy corporate culture.' *Carole Spiers*

Established in 1987, the Carole Spiers Group **(CSG)** is a leading provider of stress management and employee wellbeing services working with equal success in the contrasting cultures of the UK and the Gulf.

Through its cutting-edge stress management programmes, **CSG** has delivered benefits to both commercial and public sector clients around the world including names such as Abu Dhabi Marine Operating company, Accenture, Al Habib [Oman], Allied Bakeries, AXA, Debenhams, Dubai Cables, Etisalat, Givaudan, House of Fraser, Kanoo Group [ME], Phoenix Pharmahandel [Germany], Somerfield, W H Smith and many others.

CSG consultants have introduced personal anti-stress strategies that have been shown to improve productivity and competitive advantage decisively by encouraging a healthier corporate culture into many companies and organisations.

With a network of professional consultants, trainers and a nationwide UK Employee Counselling team, **CSG** is uniquely equipped to advise professionally on both the human and the corporate aspects of workplace stress, including bullying, intimidation, violence, post traumatic stress, redundancy, absenteeism and organisational change.

CSG is regularly called upon for professional comment by the BBC, Sky, CNN, Gulf Region TV / radio and other media, as well as being a regular contributor to Gulf News, the UK and Gulf region national press and professional journals.